C000098041

HERTFORDSHIRE
A-Z

PAMELA SHIELDS

SUTTON PUBLISHING

Sutton Publishing Limited
Phoenix Mill · Thrupp · Stroud
Gloucestershire · GL5 2BU

First published 2005

Copyright © Pamela Shields, 2005

British Library Cataloguing in Publication Data
A catalogue record for this book is available from
the British Library.

ISBN 0-7509-4250-9

Typeset in 10.5/14pt Garamond.
Typesetting and origination by
Sutton Publishing Limited.
Printed and bound in England by
J.H. Haynes & Co. Ltd, Sparkford.

To the memory of my mother,
my first and best history teacher

Contents

Introduction

At 634 square miles, Hertfordshire is one of the smallest of the English counties, with a population of around one million. Buoyant and prosperous, it has one of the strongest economies in the UK, with residents enjoying high standards of living, high per capita income and low unemployment. Home to leading pharmaceutical, bio-technology, financial services, film and computer-related businesses, it is, however, heavily dependent on the London economy.

Surrounding counties are Buckinghamshire to the west, Bedfordshire to the north, Cambridgeshire to the north-east and Essex to the east.

The original spelling of the county was Hart – the old word for stag, particularly red deer. The area referred to was around Hart Ford, mentioned in the Anglo-Saxon Chronicle of 1011, but even by then the county was already ancient. Axes and harpoons dating from 8000 BC have been found, as have cemeteries dating from 2500 BC and Iron Age settlements at Ivinghoe, Ravensburgh, Wilbury and Telegraph Hill.

The climate is so mild and dry that London doctors once advised those in poor health to move here. An old saying is: 'He who buys a home in Hertfordshire pays two years' purchase for the air.'

Although a shire, it is administered by a county council. Shire is Anglo-Saxon; county comes from the French 'comté'. Boundaries of the newly formed Norman counties corresponded with those of existing Saxon shires.

Owing to its proximity to London it was always (and still is) a popular retreat for the rich, who built grand houses with parks and gardens, which partly explains its 170 Scheduled Ancient Monuments, 110 Grade I, 472 Grade II and 7,477 listed buildings, 45 parks and gardens of special historic interest, 43 Sites of Special Scientific Interest (SSSIs) and 22 local nature reserves.

Hertfordshire has earned its place in history. This is where the Anglo-Saxons surrendered England's crown to William the Conqueror, the world-famous Tudor dynasty was born and the first manned flight was witnessed, beginning the county's long love affair with aviation.

Today, the southern border is a mere 12 miles from central London, the swiftly encroaching metropolis. Because of local government boundary changes many Hertfordshire inhabitants woke up one morning in 1965 to find they were Londoners. The natural environment is subject to constant pressures from development.

The county, served by Luton and Stansted airports, has woods, valleys, canals, lakes and open farmland. The Chilterns to the west is an Area of Outstanding Natural Beauty and more than half the county is classified as Green Belt. Inhabitants of large modern conurbations such as Stevenage and Letchworth and Welwyn Garden Cities are within walking distance of picturesque villages and historic market towns.

Hertfordshire has produced one or two actors, painters, and even a pope, but in the main the air seems to suit writers and scientists best. Poets George Chapman and William Cowper, novelists Graham Greene and W.H. Johns were born here. Writers Claud Cockburn, Maria Edgeworth and E.M. Forster were brought up here. As for scientists, among many born here are Henry Bessemer, who gave the world steel; Dr Thomas Dimsdale, who pioneered inoculation against smallpox; Sir John Bennet Lawes of artificial fertiliser fame; and William Ransom, founder of the first independent pharmaceutical company in the UK (still going strong 150 years later). Polar expedition zoologist Apsley Cherry Garrard, Professor Stephen Hawking, Joseph Lister and Sir John Sulston moved here as young children.

Authors give themselves a cut-off date for research, otherwise the book never gets written. Publishers give them a cut-off too – 50,000 words. Although I have been making jottings for eight years, my research of the county is just beginning. This is work in progress. Like the BBC, I hope it manages to educate, inform and entertain.

Abbots Langley Has gone down in history as the birthplace of Nicholas Breakspear (1100–59), the only Englishman to become pope. Born in Bedmond, he was baptised at St Lawrence the Martyr, Abbots Langley. His name is depicted on his coat of arms as a broken spear, which may refer to family skirmishes during the Norman invasion – a mere thirty-four years before his birth. Born on a farm, he ended up ruling the Vatican as Adrian IV (1154–9). There was a farm on the site of his birthplace (painting in Vatican archives) until the 1960s (plaque in Bedmond Road in front of the new houses). His father Robert became a monk at St Albans Abbey, but when Nicholas tried to join Robert he was rejected (coincidentally, Nicholas ended up in Albano, Italy). Nicholas chose the name Adrian after the pope who had sanctioned the founding of St Albans Abbey. It is thought his mother was still alive to witness her son's great achievement, but there is no record of either parent attending his coronation. His red marble sarcophagus in the crypt of St Peter's in Rome is decorated with deer skulls representing the county, roses representing England and the inscription 'Hadrianus Papa IIII'. Commemorations include plaque, St Lawrence; bust, St Saviour's; Pope, Adrian and Breakspear Roads, Abbots Langley; Nicholas Breakspear Week, Abbots Langley; Wallingford Screen, Cathedral and Abbey Church of St Alban; painting, County Hall, Hertford.

AT BEDMOND IN THIS PARISH ABOUT THE DATE OF THE BUILDING OF THIS PRESENT CHURCH WAS BORN NICHOLAS BREAKSPEAR POPE ADRIAN IV (1154-1159) THE ONLY ENGLISH POPE

THIS TABLET IS ERECTED BY THE HERTFORDSHIRE HISTORICAL ASSOCIATION · · 1924

Commemorative plaque: Nicholas Breakspear, St Lawrence the Martyr, Abbots Langley.

Addis factory, Ware Road, Hertford.

Addis, William (1734–1808) Invented the toothbrush in 1780 using pig bristles and white horsetail hairs backed onto ox bones or ivory. 1914: during the First World War every 'Tommy' was issued with a toothbrush. 1920: Addis company took over the Steam Laundry, Ware Road, Hertford, converted it into a factory and began to export all over the world. 1935: Donald Hamilton designed the Addis building in Ware Road, a pioneering example of a modern factory. Present tenants include the *Hertfordshire Mercury* (local newspaper). One of the town's major employers, Addis remained a family firm until 1996, when it was bought by Wisdom/Jordan.

Aesop's *Fables* Introduced into Britain when Alexander Neckham* of St Albans* translated them into English. Aesop, born into slavery under King Croesus in 564 BC, was sent to Delphi with gold for distribution among the citizens but, disgusted by their greed, returned it to his master. Furious locals pushed him over a cliff. He has a statue in Athens.

Agriculture 65 per cent of the county is farmland. Out of a population of almost one million just 3,500 (includes 1,794 farmers in 2005) work in agriculture. Crops include wheat, barley, beans, oilseed rape and peas. Wheat is grown for flour and feed; barley for feed and malting beer; rape for oil and feed; beans for animal feed. There are also specialist growers of apples, strawberries, blackcurrants and salad crops. The county has 33,000 sheep, 21,000 cattle and 16,000 pigs. The first crop of swedes in Britain was grown on a farm near Berkhamsted.

Alban First* Christian martyr in northern Europe, executed in 209. Offa built the abbey dedicated to him in the 700s. Albanus means 'The Briton', which is strange because he was a Roman. His real name is not known. The story goes that a Roman priest, Amphibalus, on the run for preaching Christianity, was befriended by 'Albanus', who changed clothes with him so that he could escape. Some sources say Amphibalus hid in Wales, others that his remains were found on Redbourn* Common; a priory was founded to hallow the spot and he was promoted to Saint. In the Middle Ages, to raise funds, Benedictine monks built a massive mechanical Saint Alban which said 'thank you' to those who fed it coins.

Albury Often confused with and misspelled Aldbury* even in guidebooks. In 1552 St Mary's had four bells plus the Sanctus, but one (possibly cracked) later disappeared. In 1880 another bell fell down and also disappeared. Some muttered that the devil had taken it; the more cynical said louts had dumped it in the pond 'as deep as the church spire is tall'. Albury Hall, a magnificent mansion, dominated the village for generations, but this historically important Second World War base, well known to the Germans, has been demolished. It played a vital role in Britain's survival. Special Operations Executive* agents were flown out from nearby RAF Sawbridgeworth and dropped behind enemy lines. Churchill and Eisenhower both visited the hall on a number of occasions.

Aldbury Anglo-Saxon Ald = old, bury = borough. With its backdrop of Ashridge Forest, preserving for all time a perfect picture of bygone England, Aldbury is so pretty it is almost a cliché. It made the national newspapers in the 1890s when poachers killed a gamekeeper on the Stocks* estate. Novelist Mary Ward* put the story in *Marcella*, an instant best-seller. Her next success, *Bessie Costrell*, was also about the village. Inside the fourteenth-century church

are monuments to the Duncombe family, who lived at Stocks for 500 years. The last to be buried ordered that instead of wasting money on a monument his family should use a black marble table top from the house.

Aldenham Anglo-Saxon Ald = old, ham = village. Aldenham Country Park has 175 acres. In 1973 Beatle George Harrison* bought Piggott's Manor, Hillfield Lane, for a Hindu temple. Because of traffic problems, a bypass was built for the long-suffering villagers of Letchmore Heath. Letchmore Heath is unique in Britain: during the First World War if a man who left to fight for his country failed to return, villagers put a commemorative plaque on his home. 1958: famous artist Stanley Spencer was commissioned by Aldenham School to provide a painting *The Crucifixion* for the chapel, but the school later sold it. Rare trees survive in the grounds of Haberdashers Aske School.

Alexander, Harold (1891–1969) Field Marshal Earl Alexander of Tunis, son of Earl of Caloden of Tyttenhanger*, is buried in St Margaret's, Ridge. The gravestone says simply 'Alex'. He spent childhood holidays and part of his honeymoon at Tyttenhanger. Famous for his North African campaigns against Rommel, the Second World War hero is said to have been Britain's greatest military commander since the Duke of Wellington. His funeral was held in St George's Chapel, Windsor.

America John Eliot (1604–90) of Widford* founded Harvard University; William Penn* founded Pennsylvania; Samuel Stone* founded Hartford, Connecticut; registers for the Church of St Peter and St Paul, Tring*, have entries for the ancestors of George Washington*; Jimmy Carter, 39th President of the United States, is a direct descendant of Carters from Chipperfield*; Second

World War American Air Force bases were located at Bovingdon and Nuthampstead.

Anglo-Saxon Mercia No one had heard of Mercia until Penda (d. 655) seized it from his cousin, Ceorl, in 626. *Settlements*: Benington, Berkhamsted, Caldecote, Gosmore, Hitchin, Letchworth, Offley, Pirton, Royston, St Albans, Standon, Therfield Heath, Walkern. *Churches*: Ashwell, Hitchin, Little Munden, Northchurch, Reed, St Albans (St Michael's, St Stephen's), Walkern, Westmill, Wheat-hampstead. Museums all over the county have local finds. Warrior graves under prehistoric barrows at Therfield Heath show old burial traditions were still practised by Anglo-Saxons after the introduction of Christianity. 851: King Bertwulf/Bertulph, driven out of London, relocated his headquarters to Benington*. 886: the Peace of Wedmore established the River Lea as the boundary between Wessex and the Danelaw. 895: Danes fortified the Lea (Viking sword found in the river), so King Alfred diverted it via a system of 'Waras' (weirs) – old name for Ware* – making it impassable. 912: to defend the River Lea, Alfred's son Edward the Elder founded Hertford*, which retains the Anglo-Saxon grid pattern in the street layout. It was probably at this time that Hart Ford became a 'shire' and its boundary was set. Edward also built Hertford Castle*, where the Rivers Beane and Mimram meet the Lea, as a defence against the Danes.

Anstey The lychgate of the church incorporates the old lock-up. The Norman castle was demolished by Henry III, who accused the village of being 'a nest of rebels'. Thomas Campion (1567–1620), doctor, poet and musician, was born and baptised here. He wrote masques for James I. 1944: a B-17 bomber failed to become airborne after taking off from nearby Nuthampstead airfield and crashed into the castle mound.

When the moat was drained to recover it, a door was revealed below the water line, reminding villagers of the local legend that once upon a time a local man, 'Fiddler George', went into a tunnel and was never seen again. 1972: *The Selected Songs of Thomas Campion*, edited by W.H. Auden, was published.

Architects (selected) *Lutyens*. Voysey*. Adam Brothers*: architects to George III. James Adam (1732–94) designed Shire Hall, Fore Street, Hertford* and worked on Panshanger House (demolished). His brother Robert Adam (1728–92), who designed The Priory for the Radcliffes of Hitchin*, was the driving force behind the practice, James preferring to stay at home in Hertfordshire. *Bennet and Bidwell*: Broadway Cinema, Eastcheap, Letchworth (originally had neon lighting around the entrance). *Sir Reginald Blomfield*

Shire Hall, Hertford (designed by James Adam).

The Priory, Hitchin (designed by Robert Adam).

(1856–1942): designed Abbots Langley and Little Berkhamsted war memorials, as well as Lambeth Bridge and Chequers; educated at Haileybury College*. His uncle, Sir Arthur Blomfield, designed the college chapel's enormous dome. *Edward Blore* (1787–1879): architect to William IV and Queen Victoria and of Westminster Abbey. Designed The Grove*, Watford and The Frythe, Welwyn. *William Butterfield* (1814–1900): architect of Keble College, Oxford. Rebuilt St Margaret's, Barley, which incorporated fifteenth-century screen, Jacobean pulpit, twelfth-century tower and Norman arch. He also rebuilt Holy Saviour, Hitchin, designing everything, including hinges, light fittings and heating. He disapproved of hassocks, which he said people fell over, so designed a fold-out kneeling board. *Sir Clough Williams-Ellis* (1883–1978): Portmeirion's famous architect; Sweetings, Brickendon. Leading figure in the Garden City movement and Chairman of Stevenage New Town Development Committee. *Donald Hamilton*: Addis Factory,

Ware Road, Hertford. *Nicholas Hawksmoor**. *E.B. Musman*: Comet* Hotel, St Albans Road, Hatfield, named after the de Havilland* Comet, which had just made its historic flight to Melbourne. In front is a stone pole topped by a model of the plane. *David Nye*: Rex Cinema, Berkhamsted is the best remaining example of this cinema architect's work (saved by people power*); *Sir John Soane* (1753–1837):

Comet Hotel, Hatfield (designed by E.B. Musman).

Beechwood, Flamstead; Hamels near Braughing and lodges leading to the park, Marden Hill near Hertford; Micklefield Hall, Sarratt* Tyttenhanger for the Hon. Mrs York; Kelshall Rectory near Royston* for the Revd Thomas Waddington; Wydiall Hall for Mr Heaton Ellis; North Mymms Park for the Duke of Leeds; Wall Hall for Mr G.W. Thellusson; Moor House, Rickmansworth for Mr T.H. Earle. *William Wilkins* (1778–1839): architect of the National Gallery. As a 27-year-old he designed Haileybury in 1806 for the East India Company. *Sir Christopher Wren* (1632–1723): Tring Manor for Colonel Guy; Bishop Seth Ward Almshouses, Buntingford*, are attributed to Robert Hooke, but it is thought his close friend Wren had a part in its design. Recently restored, the almshouses are still occupied. *F.R.S. Yorke* (1906–62): architect of Gatwick airport. Barclay School, Stevenage; 'Torilla', Wilkins Green Lane, Hatfield, inspired by le Corbusier and saved by the Hertfordshire Building Preservation Trust.

Arts and Crafts *Edward Burne-Jones* (1833–98): window in Hatfield church. *William Morris* (1834–96): east window, St Mary the Virgin, Rickmansworth; south window showing three archangels at St Mary's, King's Walden; south porch (1526) stained glass of the four evangelists (two on each side, may be the last of Pre-Raphaelite glass), St Mary's, Aspenden. Together Burne-Jones and Morris designed windows in St Michael and All Angels, Watford*. The painter *Patrick Heron* CBE (1920–99) was brought up in Welwyn Garden City, where he lived until 1945 (he joined Bernard Leach in St Ives). *Herbert Read** lived in Much Hadham. *Rex Whistler* (1905–44) was educated at Haileybury. He was a master of *trompe-l'oeil*, and the murals in the Tate Gallery restaurant are by him. Killed in action during the Second World War.

Ashridge In 1921, when the estate was sold, the National Trust bought 5,000 acres, much of which has open access. Rare birds, fallow deer, muntjac, badgers and the

'Torilla', Wilkins Green Lane, Hatfield (designed by F.R.S. Yorke).

now rarely found *glis glis** (dormouse) live here. The monument erected in 1832 to the 3rd Duke of Bridgewater, the Canal Duke, who once owned Ashridge, is a focal point. *Lorna Doone* was filmed here in 1934. It is said that during the Second World War General de Gaulle languished in a house on the estate writing his memoirs.

Ashridge House There has been a college on the site for 700 years. A monastery, College of Bonhommes, was founded by Edmund of Cornwall, nephew of Henry III, in 1283. When Henry VIII dissolved the religious houses, he took possession of it. Edward VI gave it to Elizabeth I, who sold it in 1579. She knew it well; she was imprisoned here when ordered to go to London to answer charges of treason against her half-sister Mary Tudor. Ill at the time, she stopped at Redbourn and North Mimms before being taken to the Tower. Her statue was taken from Ashridge in 1925 and is now in Harrow School. The present house, by James Wyatt, dates to the early nineteenth century, as do the gardens by Humphrey Repton.

Ashwell 'The well by the ash'. Source of the River Cam. Loved by poets Betjeman* and Holbrook*. Visual delights include Guildhouse, Chantry House, Town House (museum – which began with the collection of two village boys), The Maltings (flats) and a small brick house (1681 Merchant Taylors' School). Ashwell Bury, a large Victorian house remodelled by Lutyens* in the 1920s had a garden by Jekyll*. Lutyens also designed the war memorial. Famous graffiti in the church record the Black Death of 1350. The village has one of the county's remaining lock-ups, where drunks were thrown to sober up overnight. Until the early twentieth century workers were brought in to find coprolite*.

Aston Bury Moated. Built in 1540 and still inhabited in 1968, this was the famous Station XII of Special Operations Executive* fame, about which local man Des Turner wrote the definitive book. Sadly, the house has been demolished.

Aubrey, John (1626–97) Antiquarian to the Crown who discovered the megalithic remains at Avebury. His *Brief Lives* contains wonderful gossip about Bacon*, More*, Penn* and Myddelton of the New River*.

Austen, Jane (1775–1817) Novelist. Her parents, Cassandra Leigh and George Austen, had eight children, including Jane and James. James's son James Edward (1798–1874) wrote *Memoirs of Jane Austen*. 1828: when appointed curate of St Peter and St Paul, Tring, he married Emma Smith and moved to Tring Park. 1925: Sir Frank Mackintosh, writing in *Cornhill* magazine on the topography of Austen novels, said that Meryton in *Pride and Prejudice* is Hertford, where the militia talked about in the book was then based. It also had a mayor and locals carried out the occupations mentioned. The ballroom in Shire Hall resembles Meryton Assembly Rooms, where Mr Darcy first appears; he identified Longbourne, where Mr and Mrs Bennet live, a mile from Meryton, as Hertingfordbury; Charles Bingley takes Netherfield, a house on the other side of Meryton, said to be Balls Park*; Sir William Lucas is said to have lived either at Panshanger* or Goldings*. Colonel Forster, after Wickham's elopement with Lydia, makes enquiries at Barnet (in the county until 1965) and Hatfield coaching inns.

Aviation Hertfordshire was the centre of the aviation industry. When Goering said that with a week of good weather his Luftwaffe would knock England out of the war, he had not bargained on Geoffrey de Havilland* and

'New' church, Ayot St Lawrence.

Fred Handley Page*. 1784: Vincenzo Lunardi*, first* in Britain to travel by air. 1912: Captain Patrick Hamilton and Lt Atholl Wyness-Stuart, pioneer aviators, first* airmen to die serving their country. Although the granite commemoration obelisk is on the roadside

Commemoration obelisk, Willian.

between Willian and Wymondley, the tragedy happened in nearby Gravely. 1916: first* Zeppelin shot down at Cuffley. Another was shot down a month later at Potters Bar*. Sir Frank Whittle (1907–96) inventor of the jet engine in 1941, once lived at 41 Bearton Green, Hitchin. 1950s: Britain's first* aircraft museum opened behind Salisbury Hall*, London Colney.

Ayot St Lawrence One of three Ayots (Ayot Green and Ayot St Peter). Much-loved home of playwright G.B. Shaw*. Land once owned by King Harold. One lord of the manor was Sir Richard Parr, whose daughter Catherine, destined to marry Henry VIII, is said to have spent her childhood here. When Sir Lionel Lyde, a tobacco millionaire, built Ayot House in the 1770s he demolished the twelfth-century church because it spoiled his view. Forced to build a new church, he insisted it resemble the Temple of Apollo at Delos. Lyde's house, once a silk farm where material for royal christening robes was woven, was home to King Michael* of Romania.

B

Bacon, Sir Francis (1561–1626) Politician, lawyer, philosopher. Created 1st Viscount St Albans* (title extinct upon his death). Youngest son of Sir Nicholas Bacon of Gorhambury, Lord Keeper of the Great Seal under Elizabeth I, who often visited. 1601: Bacon, born in St Albans and a pupil at St Albans School, inherited the estate from his brother Anthony. Ousted from power after admitting to bribery ('I do plainly and ingenuously confess that I am guilty of corruption'), he spent the last five years of his life here, using his father's house as a base while he built himself a much grander one (cost £10,000; in today's terms over £1 million). Sir Harbottle Grimston sold it for £400 to a carpenter, who sold it on for £800. Grimston removed Bacon's coffin from St Michael's Church to make room for his own. Of the original 1568 mansion, only the porch, masonry of the Hall and one wing survive (cared for by English Heritage*).

Baldock Once pronounced Baudac, this market town, which will reclaim its old-world charm once the bypass is opened, has always been here. The main road from the A1 is on top of the ancient Icknield Way*. The town is listed by the Council for British Archaeology as being of national importance because of Iron Age and Roman settlements. 442: first recorded charter. 1142: given to the Knights Templars*. When they fell from grace it was transferred to the Knights Hospitallers*. Charles I is said to have passed through here as a prisoner. The rector brought him wine from the church in a silver chalice. Samuel Pepys* often stayed at the George and Dragon. John Bunyan* and John Wesley* also stayed there. Pepys said Baldock was full of informers who lobbied to get the town's Quakers transported. John Smith* first* to decipher Pepys's diaries, was Rector for almost forty years. Whenever George Orwell had to leave his beloved Wallington* this is the station he used. 1960s: old film studios, now Tesco, became Kayser Bondor. The Rolling Stones played there in 1963.

Balls Park Pevsner* called it 'one of the most puzzling houses of Hertfordshire'. The feet of Charles I and his son Charles II trod these halls, as did those of Cromwell. In 400 years the house was owned by just two families, and the second of those didn't arrive on the scene until 1900. The land was owned by Simon Balle MP (local school named after him) but why, in 1638 when Sir John Harrison bought it he called his mansion Balls, not Harrison's Park, is a mystery. John Evelyn* visited the Harrisons at their new house and wrote about it in his diaries. The Harrisons lived through hair-raising times. When Charles I borrowed £55,000 to pay the Scots who fought for him, Cromwell arrested Harrison and took Balls Park. Charles II returned it to the family. 1739: Lady Audrey Harrison Townshend inherited. 1899: the last Harrison Townshend died. For the first time in its history Balls Park was put up for sale. Sitting tenant Sir George Faudel Phillips bought it. 1939: home for children suffering from TB. 1941: the last Faudel Phillips died. 1947: County Council used it as a teacher-training college and appointed Monica Wingate principal. She stayed until it closed in 1970. Her brother was Orde Wingate of Chindit fame (Burma). 1979: taken over by the University

Balls Park.

of Hertfordshire. 2001: sold to a private company. Now used as a film location.

Barkway Bark = hill. Important coaching town favoured by Samuel Pepys*. The High Street is unspoiled. On its border are examples of traditional Essex weatherboarding. The 5ft-high Trinity milestone (at eye level for coach drivers) outside Barkway House is one of fifteen on the road to Cambridge. The oldest in the UK, they were financed by Dr William Warren, Master of Trinity College, in 1725 (the milestone bears the arms of Trinity College). The medieval church is said to have acoustic jars, used as amplifiers, embedded in the chancel walls. Thatched cottages 300 years old have steps up to the doors, out of reach of the once-filthy gutters. It has a seventeenth-century manor house, the eighteenth-century Red House and in the High Street behind one of the frontages lurks a medieval hall house. The Queen Anne Newsells Park was

destroyed during the Second World War and replaced by the present neo-Georgian house.

Barley Inspiration for any village in danger of losing its pub, post office or shop. The community-minded villagers raised funds for tennis courts, flashing 'Slow Down' signs, the Tudor Town House (written about by Defoe*), GP surgery, play area and nursery. 1872: St Margaret's was rebuilt by Butterfield. William Warham, one-time Rector, became the Archbishop of Canterbury who crowned Henry VIII. The village has a seventeenth-century lock-up.

Barrie, Sir James Matthew (1860–1937) Close friend of the Llewellyn Davies family of Egerton House, High Street, Berkhamsted* (now The Rex). Wrote *Peter Pan* for the five brothers. One Christmas when one brother was too ill to go to the pantomime, Barrie took it to him at Egerton House. He became their legal guardian after the tragic early deaths of their parents. One brother died in the First World War, two committed suicide. When Barrie failed to consummate his marriage, Mary, his actress wife, left him for Gilbert Cannan, a writer from Berkhamsted.

Battles Three of the most important of the fifteenth-century battles between the houses of York and Lancaster were fought here. The first battle, St Albans, opened the Wars of the Roses, the last, Barnet (in the county until 1965) ended them. 1455: at Royston, Richard, Duke of York wrote to Henry VI setting out terms for peace. Barricaded in at St Albans, Henry never received the letter. In the first so-called battle, a half-hour scuffle, Henry was taken prisoner and Richard afterwards declared himself Protector. 1461: the Second Battle of St Albans was a victory for the Lancastrians. The Yorkists left Henry under a tree on Nomansland common. Two weeks later Edward, the new Duke of York (Richard had died in battle), defeated the Lancastrians at Towton and proclaimed himself Edward IV. October 1470: Warwick, ex-head of the Yorkists, now leader of the Lancastrians, reinstated Henry VI. 1471: the Battle of Barnet could have been the third Battle of St Albans. Instead, Warwick went through to Barnet. The battle lasted four hours and ended in victory for Edward when Warwick was killed. 1740: commemorative obelisk erected, known as the Hadley Highstone. Shakespeare wrote about the battle (*Henry VI, Part III*), as did the novelist Bulwer-Lytton* in *The Last of the Barons*.

Bayford 1366: villagers asked if they could bury their dead here instead of at Essendon 3 miles away, because corpses had to be carried past a watermill on carts which often fell in the river. 1767: Sir William Baker of The Bury planted firs. A pinetum planted in the nineteenth century is now a collection of national importance with 130 species of conifer. It was restored by the John Innes

Horticultural Institution which owns part of the estate. A haven for rare birds, badgers, foxes and muntjac; there is a grotto in the grounds.

Bearskins One of the most potent of British symbols is French. Popularly called a Busby, the hats, 18in high and weighing 2lb, were taken from the heads of defeated soldiers at Waterloo. Each week Mr Green of Weston, the only master of the craft in Britain, makes eight by hand – the skin is stretched onto a wicker frame – for the Ministry of Defence. He was taught the skill in preparation for the Coronation in 1953. Five regiments wear hats made from the skins of Canadian black bears as part of their ceremonial uniform (2,500 Irish, Welsh, Scots, Coldstream and Grenadier Guards). Every year the army needs sixty-five new hats, each requiring the pelt of a black bear. Experiments with synthetic materials have been going on for twenty years but so far they have turned out the wrong colour, become distorted in the rain and wind and attract static electricity.

Beaufort, Margaret (1443–1509) Edmund (of Hadham) and Jasper (of Hatfield), sons of Owen Tudor, had joint custody of the orphaned heiress of the Duke of Somerset. Edmund, who married her when she was 12, was killed in battle when she was pregnant with their first child (Henry VII). Jasper took Margaret and the baby into his protection. No. 84 High Street, Ware, is thought to have been built by Henry VII for his mother, who was Lady of Ware Manor.

Becket, Thomas (1118–70) 1154: as Chancellor of the Exchequer was granted the Honour of Berkhamsted* Castle, where he lived in state. When he spent £800 of the King's money – unauthorised – doing it up, a furious Henry II took it back. Henry enjoyed the improvements, however, and it became one of his favourite places to stay.

Witches' hat flues.

Beer There were once big breweries in Baldock, Berkhamsted, Hatfield, Hertford, Hitchin, St Albans, Tring and Watford. Witches' hat malting flues can still be seen all over the county, especially in Ware*, once the largest brewing town in the UK. 1839: in addition to sixty-five maltings, thirty pubs in the High Street brewed on the premises. To celebrate the millennium a statue of a maltster was erected outside St Mary's. McMullen, established in 1827, is the last large independent brewer in the county. Of the 130 McMullen pubs, the first was the Greyhound at Bengeo*. Its 1891 brewery in Hartham Lane, Hertford, is still there. India Pale Ale (IPA) was dreamed up by Alexander Nowell of Much Hadham*. Going home after a day's fishing, he forgot to take the bottle of beer he had stoppered. Returning for it a few days later he found it much improved. *Et voilà!* Bottled beer. Stout* was also invented in the county.

Bengeo In 1359, when Edward*, the Black Prince, won the battles of Crécy and Poitiers, he took King John of France prisoner, put him in Hertford Castle* and allowed him

St Leonard's, Bengeo.

to live in style. While he was attending mass at St Leonard's, the King's dogs killed a pig belonging to Master Revell of Revells Hall. He paid 10s compensation. St Leonard's is thought to be the oldest church in the county. On a hill overlooking Hertford, it is sometimes open on Saturday afternoons in the summer. Bengeo is the birthplace of W.H. Johns*, creator of Biggles.

Benington Lordship. 851: King Bertwulf/ Bertulph of Mercia, driven out of London, relocated here. He held council after receiving a message from the Danes saying they had taken Canterbury and London, had 350 ships in the Thames and that Mercia was now under their control. William the Conqueror gave the lordship to Peter de Valoignes, whose son Roger built a stone keep in 1135 (demolished by Henry II in 1177). 1285: home of John de Benstede, Keeper of the Great Seal to Edward I. 1485: owned by earls of Essex. 1614: bought by Sir Julius Caesar, Chancellor of the Exchequer, Master of the Rolls to James I. 1741: bought by John Cheshire. 1832: bought by George Proctor, who built the faux Norman gatehouse, curtain wall and summerhouse with inscribed tombstone of a Greek slave. 1906: bought by Arthur Bott, an engineer. 2005: sold by Bott's grandson. Its gardens are known for their display of snowdrops and hellebores after Christmas, scillas and daffodils in spring, roses in summer and berried shrubs in autumn. They appeared in the TV series *The English Country Garden* by Rosemary Verey and are often featured in magazines (*RHS Journal, The Field, Country Life, House and Garden, Country Living*, etc.).

Berkhamsted Where the crown of England was, allegedly, offered to William the Conqueror in 1066, a date engraved on every Englishman's heart. Allegedly because William could see London – and historians

say that was doubtful from here but possible from Little Berkhamsted. Eye witnesses Guy of Amiens and William of Poitiers said the surrender took place in the hall of a Saxon fortress built over a well in Beorchehamstede. William imposed the manorial system and gave the manor to his half-brother Robert, Count of Mortain, the largest landowner in England after himself. Expecting uprisings, he told him to build a castle, the first* of a defensive ring around London. Moving on to more recent history, by 1831 the far more lucrative straw-plait industry put paid to the manufacture of fine black lace. 1866: when Lord Brownlow enclosed the common with iron railings, a local man, Augustus Smith, went to London, recruited labourers and chartered a train from Euston at the dead of night. Before dawn the railings had gone. Brownlow sued Smith but lost. 1914: the Inns of Courts Officers' Training Corps was based here. The number of celebrities, past and present, is too great to be listed. Among the most famous are William Cowper*, Clementine Churchill*, G.M. Trevelyan* and Graham Greene*. A Graham Greene Birthplace Trust Festival is held every September.

Berkhamsted Castle First* Norman castle in Britain. 1838: the main gate was demolished to build the railway line. This part of Hertfordshire was treeless and, 600ft above sea level, the castle defended the countryside as far as the eye could see. 1154: Thomas Becket* rebuilt the wooden structure in stone. Edward III gave the castle to his son, the Black Prince, when he created him Duke of Cornwall. It still belongs to the Duchy. 1495: following the death, aged 85, of Edward IV's mother Cicely Neville, Duchess of York, who lived there, it was abandoned. She was the grandmother of the ill-fated princes in the tower. 1580: the

The remains of Berkhamsted Castle.

castle was dismantled to build Berkhamsted Place*, of which nothing now remains. The castle ruins are cared for by English Heritage.

Berkhamsted Place Demolished in 1929. Built by Sir Edward Carey using masonry from the castle. A later owner was Colonel Axtell, who arranged the trial of Charles I. He was, understandably, executed at the Restoration. In the 1680s John Sayer, chef to Charles II, bought it. He also built the almshouses in the High Street.

Berners, Dame Juliana (b. 1388) Daughter of Lord Berners (there is still a Lord Berners today). Prioress of St Benedict Nunnery, Sopwell, founded in 1140. World's first* woman sports writer. Her *Boke of St Albans* (in the British Library) is about field sports, especially falconry. Her brother fought for Henry VI in the First Battle of St Albans. In the sixteenth century, after the Reformation, Sir Richard Lee (d. 1575), the King's Surveyor, bought the nunnery, demolished it and built a house on the site (remains still there). His large stone medallions with profiles of Roman generals ended up in Salisbury Hall*.

Bernhard, Prince (1911–2004) Nazi SS Officer, married Queen Juliana of the Netherlands. During the Second World War when the Germans invaded the Netherlands he took refuge in Tewin, from where, helped by Special Operations Executive*, he organised the Dutch resistance (house now owned by pop singer Marty Wilde). His later life was surrounded by scandal: he took a million-dollar bribe from Lockheed and persuaded President Perón of Argentina to buy railroad equipment from the Netherlands.

Betjeman, Sir John (1906–84) Poet Laureate. Knew the county well and wrote about it in 'Hertfordshire', 'Miss Vera Spencer Clarke', 'The Cricket Master', 'School Train', 'The Garden City', 'The Plantster's Vision', 'Group Life', 'Letchworth' and 'The Outer

Suburbs'. As a boy he was brought here reluctantly on shoots with his father. 1929: teacher at Heddon Court Prepratory School, East Barnet (then in the county). 1956: as columnist for the *Spectator* he wrote in praise of Ashwell* and returned to make a video. Considering his self-confessed loathing of modern architecture, it is a mystery why, in 1974, he agreed to open Campus West, Welwyn Garden City.

Bishop's Stortford The River Stort took its name from the town, not the other way round. William the Conqueror built wooden Waytemore Castle. It was rebuilt with stone in the twelfth century. 1208: King John destroyed it, then rebuilt it. By 1549 it was in ruins and was gone by 1649. In the 1400s Dick Whittington (d. 1423), lord of nearby Thorley, extended the manor house. Prosperity came from the town's malting industry, which improved with the opening of the Stort Navigation in 1769, the coaching trade and the arrival of the railways. Walter Gilbey* of gin fame was born here, as was Cecil Rhodes*, founder of Rhodesia, whose home is now a museum. Today all that is left of the castle is a mound, but the town still has many old buildings. Parts of the George, where Charles II is said to have stayed with Nell Gwyn, date from the fourteenth century.

Black Squirrels Peculiar to the county. If you go to Norton Common, Letchworth* or Ashridge*, you may see one. They are, apparently, easily recognisable, with scraggy, not bushy, tails.

Bleak House Dickens stayed in the Queens Hotel, Chequer Street, St Albans while writing the book. The house is thought to be either the Georgian mansion, Gombards, on the corner of Catherine Street and Normandy Road (once known as Altons Folly, it is in the right place but looks wrong) or, more probably, the seventeenth-century

Great Nast Hyde.

Great Nast Hyde, known locally as Bleak House, off the St Albans to Hatfield road.

Blondin, Jean née Gravelet (1824–97) Took the name from a circus owner he worked for in France. 1859: he practised his tightrope act across the Mimram Valley before perfecting it across Niagara Falls. Why the Mimram? This is where he taught fellow high-wire enthusiast, his friend George Dering of Lockleys (now a school), near Welwyn. Blondin loved England and settled in Ealing.

Blue Streak Built by de Havilland*. 1953: a bankrupt, war-weary Britain found itself threatened again in the Cold War by the USSR. 1954: Duncan Sandys (Winston Churchill's son-in-law), Minister of Supply, cooperated with America to build a missile with a 2,000-mile range and a thermonuclear warhead. 1957: White Paper on defence abolished conscription and cancelled new aircraft, so as to fund nuclear weapons. De Havilland won the contract to build the British Intercontinental Ballistic Missile, Blue Streak. Rolls-Royce built the engines. 1960: Polaris submarines took over. Blue Streak continued as a satellite launcher until 1972. One ended up in the hands of a farmer who used its huge fuel tanks to house his chickens; another in a museum in Scotland.

Body Shop Ransom's of Hitchin brew the magic potions for the one-time icon of the High Street. Sainsbury's car park often smelled of dewberry. Behind the plaque of 105 Bancroft, a delightful fourteenth-century gatehouse, lies the fascinating story of the first* independent pharmaceutical chemist in Britain. William Ransom started what it still does today – extracting plant material for the healthcare, food, beverage and cosmetic industries – some 150 years ago.

Boleyn, Anne (1507–36) Before becoming Queen she is said to have gone on a retreat at Sopwell nunnery. As she was hated by Londoners loyal to Queen Catherine, it is thought her secret marriage to Henry VIII took place in the chapel there. She also stayed in the Dower House, Ayot St Lawrence, The Bury, Gadebridge Park, Hemel Hempstead, Hertford Castle and Moor Park, Rickmansworth.

Boleyn, Mary (1505–43) Henry VIII had love affairs with Elizabeth Howard and her stepdaughters Mary and Anne Boleyn. Pregnant by Henry VIII in 1521, Mary was married off to the penniless Sir William Carey, a willing accomplice. Her second child, Catherine, is also believed to have been Henry's. Mary and William accompanied Henry to the Field of the Cloth of Gold in France. Catherine of Aragon and her daughter Princess Mary stayed with Mary and William at Hunsdon*. After Carey died of the plague and Mary married William Stafford, Henry VIII brought up her two children with his others.

Borehamwood One of the oldest centres of the UK's film industry; you can't help but wonder whether locals resent the fact that Elstree gets the glory. Known as the British Hollywood, Elstree Film Studios*, now 100 years old, are here, not at Elstree. This is where Hitchcock made the first British talkie, *Blackmail*, in 1929. 1996: when the studios were threatened with closure Hertsmere Council purchased them and with local support transformed them to today's state-of-the-art film mecca. The *Borehamwood Times* online has wonderfully gossipy showbiz snippets from the good old (film) days.

Bottoms Hertfordshire is a gift to schoolchildren. It has fifty Bottoms for them to giggle over. Among many favourites are Claggy, Holy and Largess.

Boudicca (Welsh) or Boadicea (Latin) Queen of the Brythons (Britons). AD 61: the

Elstree Film Studios, Borehamwood.

most serious rebellion the Romans faced in Britain almost ended their domination after a mere seventeen years. With the neighbouring Trinovantes tribe Boudicca amassed an army. Once she could have called on the Catuvellauni*, but they had sold out to the enemy by taking Roman citizenship, and the town they had founded, Verulamium (after the River Ver), the third largest in Britain, was under Roman rule. Boudicca advanced on Verulamium with such force that the Roman generals who went to help turned back. The city was sacked and it was many years before it recovered. Verulamium was renamed St Albans following the founding of the abbey by Offa*.

Bovingdon Bufan Dune, 'above the hill'. Famous 'revels' in June. The Bull Inn may have been the hideout of a wartime spy (radio transmitter found in the attic, 1985). HM Prison, The Mount, is on what was a major US Air Force station. At 500ft and flat – well suited for flying – it was used by Eighth Air Force, principally as a B-17 (Flying Fortress) training base. Clark Gable, James Stewart, Steve McQueen and William Holden all flew from here as airmen. Glen Miller, Bob Hope, Eleanor Roosevelt and General Eisenhower visited. 1946: RAF resumed control. 1951: USAF until 1962. A Mosquito landed during filming of *633 Squadron*. Also filmed here: TV's *The Avengers, Blakes 7* and in the 1970s Harrison Ford's *Hanover Street*. 1969: Ministry of Defence property sold. The original tower just outside the main prison fence can be seen on Saturdays by going to the market on one of the runways. 1972: the village made headlines when Graham Young, who worked for Hadland Phototronics, was sentenced to life at St Albans Crown Court for poisoning his work colleagues. His life story is immortalised in the film *The Young*

Poisoner's Handbook. In 1962, aged 14, having poisoned his stepmother and attempted to poison his father, sister and a schoolfriend, he was committed to Broadmoor as criminally insane. Although he studied poisons while there and became an expert, he was proclaimed cured after nine years and discharged. He told a nurse on leaving that he intended to kill one person for every year he had been detained. He was sent to a government training centre, where he poisoned 34-year-old Trevor Sparkes (not fatally) before applying for and getting a job in Bovingdon. Almost immediately employees started to fall ill from a 'Bovingdon Bug'. Young had poisoned their tea. Storeroom manager Bob Egle and distribution manager Fred Biggs died, Jethro Batt and David Tilson survived. 1990: Young died in suspicious circumstances in Parkhurst Prison, aged 42.

Bowen, Elizabeth (1899–1973) Novelist. Her father, an Anglo-Irish aristocrat, died young. 1912: her mother, Florence Colley, died of cancer, her aunt died of TB and her uncle went down with the *Titanic*. Elizabeth was sent to live in Harpenden* with Laura, her mother's remaining sister, who kept house for the remaining brother, the Revd Wingfield Colley, curate at St John's. The semi-detached house, South View, was where Elizabeth, a pupil of Harpenden Hall School, wrote her first story. Her short story *The Little Girls* is about her time there. She was a close friend of the Buchans* and godmother to their first son, William (present Lord Tweedsmuir).

Bowes-Lyon The Gilberts of The Bury, St Paul's Walden, married into the Bowes family. When Mary Bowes married into the Lyon family (Earl of Strathmore) she kept her maiden name and became Bowes-Lyon. Lady Elizabeth* Bowes-Lyon and her brother David, youngest of the ten children of the

Earl of Strathmore, spent much of their childhood at St Paul's Waldenbury*.

Boxmoor 1790s: Grand Junction Canal. 1804: brothers Henry and Sealy Fourdrinier built the first* paper-making machine at Frogmore Mill on the Gade. For many years it was the only type available, and today many still bear the name. Nineteenth century: when the postman was robbed of his mailbag, a local man, Snooks, immediately left for Southwark. He sent a servant to the shop, telling her to make sure she got the right change from his £5 note, but had in fact given her £50, which aroused suspicion with the trader, who reported it. Snooks, found guilty at Hertford Assizes, was hanged on Boxmoor Common on 11 March 1802; the day was declared a public holiday. He offered his gold watch to anyone prepared to give him a decent burial, but his offer was not accepted. After he had been hanged from a tree the executioner cut him down and started to remove Snooks's clothes (a hangman's perk) but was stopped. Locals subscribed to a wooden coffin. A white stone opposite the entrance to a school (just past the station under a bridge in a field) marks the spot. It is thought that he was the last highwayman to be hanged in England.

Boxmoor Common 1574: Elizabeth I* gave the land to love of her life Robert Dudley, Earl of Leicester. After he died it was conveyed to sixty-seven named inhabitants of Hemel Hempstead and Bovingdon to safeguard grazing and fishing rights. Over the years, the sixty-seven grew to 80,000, represented by twelve elected. 1794: trustees sold 25 acres for the building of the Grand Union Canal. The money bought Boxmoor Wharf, Sheethanger and Roughdown Commons, home to rare insects and flowers. 1809: Boxmoor Trust founded and twelve Trustees appointed. The Trust financed

Belted Galloways on Boxmoor Common.

Boxmoor Hall and the Old Town Hall, now arts centres. One of the Trust's meadows, where Kodak now stands, was exchanged for land at Chaulden Meadows. The Water Gardens were built on Trust land. 1970s: Belted Galloway cattle were brought from the Scottish Borders to maintain the moor. 1965: rare Norfolk Horn black-faced sheep had died out, with one ram left at Whipsnade Zoo. Back breeding was used to revive the breed. 1993: in conjunction with the Rare Breeds Survival Trust the Trust bought two of the sheep (now 100). Numbers of larks in the UK are falling, but there are six pairs here despite the presence of kestrel, falcon, sparrowhawk and, on rare occasions, red kite and buzzard. Little and tawny owls nest here and attempts are made to encourage barn owls.

Bramfield Needing the Church in his pocket, Henry II persuaded Chancellor Thomas Becket to become a clergyman and gave him his first living – St Andrew's. 1782: posing as a pieman, Walter Clibbon went to local markets to spot those who had done well enough to warrant an ambush. On Saturday 28 December at Hertford market

Clibbon's Post, Bramfield.

Robert Whittenbury took £200 and fought off Clibbon to keep it. Clibbon was hanged on the site of his attack. His grave is marked by a tall post (replaced several times) on Bull Green Road between Bramfield and Datchworth.

Braughing Pronounced Braffing. This popular film location is known for sausages, Old Man's Day and as the one-time secret hidey-hole of lovers H.G. Wells and Rebecca West*. Old Man's Day is 2 October. Four hundred years ago Matthew Wall of Fleece Lane died young. As his coffin was carried to church, a pallbearer slipped, causing it to shake, and Matthew revived. By the terms of his will on the anniversary of his 'funeral' children still sweep Fleece Lane, while bells toll and a song written for the occasion is sung in the graveyard. 1964: the railway station fell to Dr Beeching's axe and is still much missed.

Breachwood Green Under the flight path of aircraft from Luton Airport. 2004: villagers walked to the airport to protest over its expansion. 1678: John Bunyan* preached from the pulpit in the Baptist Chapel. It owns a 'Breeches' Bible, so called because translators in 1560 preferred the word 'breeches' to 'aprons' (Genesis says Adam and Eve sewed fig leaves together to make themselves aprons); also known as the Geneva Bible, as its Protestant translators settled there to escape persecution under Mary Tudor. Shakespeare owned one, as did Cromwell. The south window in the church, by William Morris, depicts three archangels. The village school built in 1859 was a straw-plait school for fifty children who worked a ten-hour day leavened (sic) by Bible readings. In 2004 a villager posted her memories on a website recording long-gone Christmas customs: because the area had no conifers, a holly branch was decorated with coloured ribbons; for breakfast on Christmas morning children were treated to a 'collop' (thick round slice) of home-cured ham and 'snapdragons', raisins soaked in rum overnight, dried and eaten like sweets.

Brickendon Henry II gave the manor to St Albans Abbey in part expiation for the murder of Becket and granted it special privileges and rights. Once known as Brickendon Green, it has won Village of the Year contests many times. Its peace is under threat from the proposed expansions of Stansted and Luton airports. 1894: 450 Roman denarii from the third century discovered. 1919: another 45 coins found. 1962: the 'Brickendonbury Hoard' was stolen from Hertford Museum and has not been seen since. 1914–18: wounded soldiers convalesced in the Military Hospital at Bricket House. 1929: Britain's first naturist* camp opened in Bricket Wood. 1939: during the Second World War Brickendonbury was Special Operations Executive* Station 17. A propaganda film entitled *Now It Can Be Told* was shot at Brickendonbury at the end of the war and a 1980s documentary *The Secret War* showed archive footage from the estate. Stories on the village website include one about Mrs Barclay of Fanshawe's. When trains and cars brought visitors from London after the war, she was astonished to find a family on her lawn having a picnic. She found out where they lived and the following week she picnicked in their garden. The poet Stevie Smith* wrote 'Brickenden', bemoaning the fact that its stream had dried up and she, out walking, was thirsty. Broxbourne Woods, at 586 acres, is the largest woodland area in the county, with most of it within the parish.

British Film Institute The BFI at Kingshill Way, Berkhamsted, sets the world standard for film preservation and restoration.

The British Schools, Queen Street, Hitchin.

Collections started in the 1940s include half a million films and TV programmes recording British life since the invention of cinema. 1987: John Paul Getty Jnr funded the Conservation Centre. 1994: workmen in Blackburn found rusty metal drums containing 800 rolls of nitrate film in the cellar of the old studios of Mitchell and Kenyon who, 150 years ago, toured Britain capturing working-class life on film. That they are clear, sharp and unscratched is thanks to ten years of BFI work (see the BBC2 series). This is the only place where you can see Betjeman's lost 1973 film *Metroland*.

Blue Plaque on the British Schools, Hitchin.

British Schools Museum Plaque in Queen Street, Hitchin, charts the history of education from 1810 to 1969. Matthew Arnold, inspector of schools, visited in 1851. The rare Lancasterian schoolroom was built in 1837 for the Monitorial System – one master taught 300 boys with the aid of 30 monitors. Advocated in 1804 by Joseph

Lancaster, the system spread all over the world. The school also has a rare Victorian galleried classroom. A local woman, Jill Grey, managed to get it listed, Mr Brian Limbrick overturned its sale and volunteers keep it going. It now has Registered Museum status.

Brocket Hall The first Brocket called his home after himself, the second called himself after his house. The first house was built by Sir John Brocket in the sixteenth century. The second and present house, now a conference centre, is steeped in scandal. It was built in 1760 for Sir Mathew Lamb MP (1705–68), whose wife was one of the many mistresses of the Prince Regent. A frequent visitor, he stayed in the Prince Regent Suite. Their first son, Penistone, held wild parties at the Hall and built a racecourse for the Prince. Second son, the sober William, inherited the estate from his brother and became Lord Melbourne, husband of the notorious Lady Caroline Lamb*. Melbourne was PM to Queen Victoria, who stayed at the Hall. 1848: when William died childless, his sister Emily Lamb inherited. Her lover, Henry Temple, Lord Palmerston (1784–1865), whom she later married, is said to have died of a heart attack at Brocket *in flagrante delicto* with a chambermaid. 1921: after the First World War Charlie Nall Cain, a Liverpool brewer, bought Brocket, wangled a knighthood and reinvented himself as Sir Charles. 1933: he wangled a peerage, bought a Grant of Arms and called himself Lord Brocket. 1934: the estate was inherited by his son Arthur Nall Cain (1904–67), anti-Semite devotee of Hitler, who hosted meetings for Nazi supporters here. 1996: his grandson, Charles Nall Cain, was sent to Springhill Prison, convicted of fraud after claiming on his insurance for three 'stolen' (*sic*) Ferrari cars and one Maserati. Margaret Thatcher stayed at the Hall while writing her memoirs. Christophe Novelli, famous French chef, has his restaurant, Auberge du Lac, in an eighteenth-century hunting lodge on the estate. Film location for (among many) *Lady Caroline Lamb* (1972) with Sarah Miles, Richard Chamberlain, John Mills, Sir Ralph Richardson; *Willow* (1988) with Val Kilmer and Joanne Whalley; *A Kiss before Dying* (1991); *Pride and Prejudice* (1995), with Colin Firth as Darcy in his famous wet shirt.

Brookmans Park Known for personalised number plates, golf courses and the first* regional wireless transmitter. 1929: BBC London Regional Wireless Station paid £10,000 for Lot 5 of the newly broken-up estate. The whole scheme cost £130,500. 1947: first* twin transmitter station in the world capable of broadcasting programmes simultaneously. 21 October 1929: first regional programme. 9 March 1930: simultaneous programme on the national service. The original Marconi transmitters were in use until the Second World War, powered by diesel generators until connected to the national grid in 1939. Capable of transmitting on two waves simultaneously, it became possible to transmit sound and vision. 30 March 1930: television tests were made using thirty-line pictures, the first* public transmission of simultaneous sound and vision in Britain (and probably in the world). Locals used filters on TVs and telephones to avoid picking up radio programmes, but could not prevent signals being picked up by central-heating radiators. Changing from analogue to digital removed the interference.

Broxbourne Brock = badger, bourne = stream. When the A10 road was built, a tunnel was provided for the badgers. 1198: the manor was owned by the Knights Hospitallers*. Following his closure of religious houses, Henry VIII granted the manor to their bailiff, John Cock of Tewin. He became Sheriff of Hertfordshire in 1548 and Keeper of the Wardrobe to Elizabeth I and James I. His son Henry entertained James here to introduce him to the English nobility while on his way to London to claim the throne in 1603. 1946: manor house and grounds bought by County Council (Golf and Country Club). In St Augustine's church there is a monument to John McAdam*. Even more interesting is one to Edward Christian*, brother of the famous mutineer.

Buchan, John (1875–1940) As an Oxford undergraduate he spent weekends with his friend Auberon Herbert, nephew of Lord Cowper, at Panshanger. Buchan married Susan Grosvenor (related to the Duke of Westminster), who spent much of her childhood at Moor Park*. During the First World War Buchan was probably an intelligence gatherer at Letchworth*.

Bulwer-Lytton, Lord Edward (1803–73) Of Knebworth House*, buried in Poets' Corner, Westminster Abbey. One of Victorian England's most popular novelists, close friend of Dickens. 'It was a dark and stormy night' opened *Paul Clifford*. He also said: 'The pen is mightier than the sword.' Although he was ridiculed by London literati, his novels sold on a par with those of Dickens. The only books not slammed by the critics were *Pelham* and *Eugene Aram*, although Trollope* said he was unable to finish them. *The Coming Race*, a pioneer work of sci-fi, has a cult following. The 'race' possessed a mysterious source of power, 'Vril', which led to a marketing brainwave. An entrepreneur combined Vril with meat extract and sold it as Bo(vine)vril. His novel *Rienzi*, adapted by Wagner, thrilled Hitler, who could relate to Rienzi establishing a republic and restoring pride to Rome. Hitler said: 'In that hour it began.' Edward met his wife Rosina* through ex-paramour Lady Caroline Lamb*.

Bulwer-Lytton, Lady Rosina (1802–82) It is unlikely anyone would have heard of her had she not married Bulwer-Lytton. She followed her mentor Lady Caroline Lamb's* example and turned her disastrous life into *Cheveley*, a libellous account of her marriage. When Bulwer-Lytton tried to get her committed to an asylum, she was befriended by Fanny Trollope*.

Buntingford Protected town centre with lovely old buildings dating from the fifteenth century. The earliest mention of it is as Buntas Ford in 1185, concerning land owned by the Templars*. Attractions include a sixteenth-century turret clock with one hand and the almshouses of 1684, built by townsman Bishop Seth Ward, mathematician and astronomer. Until the 1660s clocks had only one elaborate hour hand, but a minute hand has been added to many, so this one is now very rare. The height of the town's

8 a.m. Rare one-hand turret clock, Buntingford.

prosperity came with the stagecoach. Many inns opened to cater for travellers on their way north via Ermine Street. Samuel Pepys's* wife became unwell while staying at a local inn. The famous Mr Hobson* who gave customers no choice was born here and left money to the town. As residents became prosperous and bought cars, the railway station fell to the Beeching axe (1963).

Bunyan, John (1628–88) Preacher. Although Bunyan's aunt Alice lived in Hitchin* and his sister Elizabeth had been baptised at St Mary's, the incumbent tried to ban him from preaching in the town. A member of the Baptist church in Kensworth (then in Herts), he preached all over the county. Stayed at Castle Farm, Preston, with the Foster brothers. In Gosmore is Bunyan's Dell, a natural amphitheatre in Wain Wood where he preached secretly to thousands. Bunyan also preached in a cottage at Coleman Green between Sandridge and Waterend. The only contemporary portrait (now in the National Portrait Gallery), painted in 1684 when he was 56, was found in a cottage in Codicote. 1674: Agnes Beaumont was wrongly accused of poisoning her father so that she could be with Bunyan. She is buried in the graveyard of Upper Tilehouse Street Baptist church, Hitchin, where Bunyan preached.

Burton, Sir Richard (1821–90) Explorer, and translator of the *Arabian Nights*. Brought up in Barham House (renamed Boreham) Elstree*, out of which he was (to his mind) cheated because of his mother's (to him) misplaced loyalty. His maternal grandfather, Richard Baker, intended to leave his fortune to his favourite grandson (Richard Burton), but Burton's mother persuaded her father to leave it instead to his first son, Richard Baker Jnr, her half-brother (Richard Baker married twice), whom she worshipped. As it was worth £80,000 and as her half-brother gambled it all away, Burton never forgave his mother.

Bushey St James's was restored in 1871 by Sir Gilbert Scott*, who added the aisles and porch. The pulpit has been here since 1606, when James I ordered one to be erected in every church. The sounding board above means the preacher's words are not lost in the rafters, but bounce down towards the congregation. In the 1720s Daniel Defoe*, riding over Bushey Heath, was 'surprised at the beauty . . . a planted garden . . . one grand parterre . . .'. What would he think now? Sir Hubert von Herkomer, who had an art school and film studios in Melbourne Road, is buried in the churchyard. His name is not as well known as his paintings, e.g., *On Strike*, showing a labourer with his wife and baby in the doorway of their Bushey cottage. The local British Legion must surely have Britain's most imposing entrance. It once led to Herkomer's Bavarian schloss, which cost him £75,000 in 1894. Bushey Hall was Station 361 during the Second World War. Lysanders, Hurricanes and Spitfires all took off from here until October 1942, when the US Air Force took over.

Byron, Lord (1788–1824) With Lady Caroline Lamb*, held centre stage in a debauched Regency society. Before *Childe Harold* was published he was persona non grata, so needed Caroline (she read the proofs) and wrote ten times a day asking her to run away with him. Lady Melbourne*, her mother-in-law, encouraged him to marry her niece. When he told Caroline, she tried to kill herself.

Caesar, Julius (100–44 BC) Roman dictator. Made two expeditions to Britain, 55 and 54 BC, to see whether it was worth conquering. With 800 ships and 35,000 soldiers, he didn't find it difficult to defeat the Cassivellauni* at Wheathampstead*.

Campaign for the Protection of Rural England (CPRE)/The Hertfordshire Society runs the Best Kept Village (formerly Village of the Year) competitions to nurture pride of place. Without the CPRE, folk might wake up one day to find they live in Luton or London.

Canterbury Tales One of the world's most famous pilgrimages. Chaucer's* real-life Doctor of Physick in the Prologue was from Gaddesden* and the Cook came from Ware*. His patron and childhood friend was John of Gaunt, who lived in Hertford Castle*. *The Book of the Duchesse* is an elegy for Gaunt's wife Blanche, who died of the plague. In it the narrator, strolling through a wood, stumbles upon John, a mysterious, mournful man in black.

Canute, King (994–1035) Based his Royal Mint at Hertford. Tovi the Proud of Hitchin, his standard-bearer, built a stone cross at Waltham, and it may be that the town's name refers to this cross, not to Eleanor's*.

Cartland, Barbara (1901–2000) Writer. *Guinness Book of Records*: world's best-selling author. President, St John Ambulance. 1950: bought Camfield Place, Essendon, with 400 acres and moved in with a butler, chef, lady's maid and a comptroller of the household.

County councillor until she had the law changed to force local councils to provide sites for gypsies (PM John Major scrapped it). Established a camp in her grounds called Barbaraville. Campaigned for better conditions in care homes for the elderly, better pay for nurses and midwives and against chemical pollution. Buried under an oak tree in her garden, in a cardboard coffin.

Cassiobury House demolished in 1927, stables now a retirement home. Family seat of Arthur Capel, Earl of Essex, a Royalist, executed at the same time as Charles I. His heart, presented to Charles II, found its way back here in 1809. Where is it now? His son, also Arthur Capel, Earl of Essex, anti-Royalist, committed suicide in the Tower of London, where he was imprisoned for his involvement in the Rye* House Plot against Charles II. Queen Adelaide lived here in 1846 and was visited by Queen Victoria and the Prince of Wales (Edward VII).

Cassivellauni Celtic tribe. 55 BC headquartered at Wheathampstead, a settlement of mud and wattle huts on the hilltop. When Julius Caesar demolished the settlement, the tribe moved to what became Verulamium (St Albans), until Boudicca* demolished that too.

Cassivellaunus Welsh for 'expert warrior'. 55 BC defeated at Wheathampstead by Julius Caesar. His life was spared, but he had to send hostages to Rome, pay an annual tribute and make an agreement refraining from making war on the pro-Rome Trinovantes tribe in the south.

Catechism Written by Alexander Nowell (1507–1602), Dean of St Paul's, Rector of St Andrew's, Much Hadham*, and printed in the Prayer Book of 1549. Elizabeth I scolded him for giving her a prayer book full of saints and martyrs, and once, when he was preaching, she called out: 'Leave that.

We have heard enough.' He was so upset he could not continue.

Cathcart, Lady Elizabeth (1699–1783) Star of Maria Edgeworth's *Castle Rackrent*. Lizzie Malyn, daughter of a Southwark brewer, married Squire Fleet of Tewin Water for his money. Her second husband, Captain Sabine of Queen Hoo Hall, Tewin, was the love of her life. Her third husband was Charles, Lord Cathcart, whom she married in 1739 for his title. In 1745 her fourth husband, Colonel Hugh McGuire, an Irish psychopath, married her for her money and incarcerated her for twenty years on his estate in Ireland. He died in a duel in 1764, when she was 65. She came home and enjoyed the Revd Edward Young's* Spa Assembly Rooms, where she used to dance until in her eighties. Buried in St Peter's in a vault near her first husband. She left money for the celebration of a huge funeral feast.

Catherine of Aragon 1524: held court at Hertford Castle. While Henry was trying to divorce her she stayed with the sympathetic Cardinal Wolsey* at Moor Park*.

Catherine de Valois Wife of Henry V. As a young widow, when her son Henry was 8 months old, she secretly married her servant, Owen Tudor*. The Frenchwoman and the Welshman between them founded England's most famous dynasty in Much Hadham*.

Champneys Wigginton. 1925: Britain's first* nature cure resort, opened by Dr Stanley Lief (1892–1963) when he bought the mansion (built in 1307 by Ralph de Champneys) from the Rothschilds. It swiftly became a mecca for the rich (still is). He devised treatments based around fasting, saying it was necessary to eliminate toxins from the body, and pioneered the concept of holistic health, treating the whole person: mind, body and soul.

Chapman, Eddie (1920–97) Aka Wearside, aka Zigzag. Wartime double agent sent over from the occupied Channel Isles to sabotage the Mosquito assembly line at London Colney, for which he was awarded the Iron Cross by Hitler. After the war he was rumoured to be involved with the Kray Brothers. Until 1980 he ran a health farm in Rectory Lane, Shenley. He probably knew that Shenley was part of the north London defence system. A massive anti-tank ditch is still connected to many old pillbox gun emplacements. Chapman was played in the film *Triple Cross* (1967) by Christopher Plummer.

Chapman, George (1599–1634) Poet and playwright. Born and brought up in Tilehouse Street, Hitchin*. Said to be the rival poet in Shakespeare's *Sonnets*. First* translator into English of Homer. Tribute by John Keats, 'On First Looking into Chapman's Homer'. Wrote 'Eastward Ho' with Ben Jonson and was thrown into prison for libel. A member of Sir Walter Raleigh's inner circle.

Charles I (1600–49) When his father James I died at Theobalds*, Charles was proclaimed King at the gates of Cedars Park, Cheshunt. He also often stayed at his father's house in Royston*. At Theobalds he received petitions from parliament and left from there to head his army. He hid all over the county in disguise, including at Wheathampstead, before riding on to Stevenage, Baldock and Royston on his way north to meet the Scots. The Bury, Rickmansworth, was also one of his hidey-holes. 26 June 1647: taken prisoner while staying at Royston.

Charlton House Opposite the Windmill pub. Plaque. Henry Bessemer (1813–89) was born and brought up here and often reminisced about his idyllic childhood. He learned metallurgy in his father's type

Remains of James I's palace, Royston.

foundry; his godfather was Henry Caslon of type font fame. Numerous inventions, e.g. typesetting machine. During the Crimean War Bessemer patented a process by which pig iron could be turned into steel. It revolutionised the world. The Bessemer Converter at Kelham Island Museum, Sheffield, is one of only three remaining. Within twenty years, Sheffield was producing 10,000 tons of Bessemer steel every week, a quarter of the UK output. The invention was not superseded until 1974.

Chaucer, Geoffrey (1340–1400) Author of *Canterbury Tales**. Richard II appointed Chaucer Clerk of the Works responsible for main-tenance of all royal buildings such as Tower of London, Palace of Westminster, Windsor Castle, Berkhamsted Castle* and King's Langley* Palace. Langley was vast, almost as grand as the Palace of Westminster.

Edward III and Richard II both lived at Langley, which featured in Shakespeare's *Richard II*. Friend of John of Gaddesden*.

Cherry Garrard, Apsley (1886–1969) Polar explorer, lived in Lamer*, near Wheathampstead*. Befriended by G.B. Shaw, whose garden abutted his grounds. Buried in nearby St Helen's churchyard (statuette inside). Zoologist to Captain Scott's last expedition in 1911, he reached the One Ton depot where he waited in vain. He led the party that found their bodies just 11 miles from the safety of a huge food cache. His autobiography *The Worst Journey in the World* refers to a different journey. In almost total darkness and temperatures of −70°, he, Bill Wilson and Henry Bowers hauled their sledge to the far side of Ross Island to take an egg from the Emperor penguin rookery.

Cheshire, Leonard (1917–92) Baron. VC. National hero, one of the most famous airmen of the Second World War, married Sue Ryder*. Established one of his Homes in Hitchin at a time when the disabled were excluded from mainstream society. The youngest Group Captain in the RAF, he developed low-level bombing techniques, but was so sickened by what he saw that after the war he dedicated his life to working for world peace. Lifelong member of the Campaign for Nuclear Disarmament (CND).

Cheshunt William Cecil, Lord Burghley, built the magnificent Theobalds* Palace (Tibbalds) in 1563. Only parts remain, following its destruction by Cromwell. James I* obtained it in exchange for a string of old ruins, including Hatfield*. This is where he died and where his son, the ill-fated Charles I, was proclaimed king. Theobalds Park, built in 1763 by the Meux family, is still here. Grove Cottage, where Bishop's Court stands, was, it is thought, the inspiration for Anthony Trollope's *Small House at Allington* (photograph in Cheshunt Library).

Chipperfield No known link with the circus family. In a recent TV programme a local farmer said that his farm is the nearest one to Piccadilly Circus. He also said the farmer was once the richest man in the village, but today is among the poorest. The village has strong links with Jimmy Carter, 39th President of the USA. The farmer's son, born in 1924, is, according to *Debrett's Peerage*, a direct descendant of local Carters. Many were dissenters, which may be why brothers Thomas and John emigrated to America on the *Safety* in 1635. John bought farmland and his son Robert, nicknamed 'King Carter', was one of America's first millionaires. The village has connections with two other famous names: Sidney Paget,

illustrator of Conan Doyle's Sherlock Holmes* books, lived in Braziers on Tower Hill. For an illustration in *Rodney Stone*, he persuaded the blacksmith at Forge Cottage to work at night and arranged for locals in the high hats of the period to stand around the fire. 1959: Peter Sellers bought the manor house. 1838: St Paul's, on the beautiful common with Apostles' Pond and ancient sweet chestnuts, was built by public subscription. 2000: locals raised £350,000 to build the adjoining room.

Chorleywood Churl = common man – we still say churlish. Given to St Albans Abbey by Offa* when Shire Lane was the boundary between Wessex and Mercia. King John's Farm Friends Meeting House is where William Penn* married in 1672. This is a stop on London's Metropolitan line, part of the Metroland so loved by John Betjeman*.

Christian, Edward (1758–1823) Elder brother of Fletcher Christian, *Bounty* mutineer. Professor of Law at Cambridge University, he lived in Broxbourne* (monument in St Augustine's). Captain Bligh was exonerated from blame until 1792, when Edward interviewed survivors of the *Bounty* in front of a panel which stated that Bligh's behaviour went beyond the acceptable norms of command. Edward impressed his audience, especially William Wordsworth, on whose behalf he later acted. Bligh was vilified after Edward published the minutes of the proceedings, which painted a picture of him as a tyrant. Edward had another brother, Charles, younger than Fletcher, a surgeon on a West Indies Company ship. Several months before the *Bounty* sailed from Portsmouth, Charles was involved in a mutiny on his ship, as a result of which he was banned from sailing for two years. It is thought that Fletcher was well aware of his brother's actions.

Churches (selection) *Caldecote*: St Mary Magdalene. Fourteenth century. Maintained by Friends of Friendless Churches. Grade II*. *Flamstead**: St Leonard's. Medieval wall paintings of *St Christopher, Christ in Glory* and *The Last Supper*, discovered in 1932. Pevsner said they are of great importance. *Hitchin*: St Mary's. Largest in the county, founded by Offa* in 792 before he founded St Albans Abbey. 1115: it was hit by a hurricane and rebuilt. 1298: the roof caved in after an earthquake. Rebuilt. *Hexton*: St Faith. Double-decker pulpit, manorial pew with a fireplace. *Ridge*: St Margaret's. Grade II*. Hertfordshire puddingstone, fifteenth-century wall painting of St Christopher. Buried in the churchyard is wartime leader Alexander* of Tunis. *Thorley*: St James the Great. Twelfth-century marble font large enough for immersion of a baby at baptism; Cromwell's men gave it to a local farm to be used as an animal drinking trough. 1855: the font was restored to its original use. Tower with thin eight-sided Hertfordshire* Spike was used in the war to watch for the night-flying Lysander aircraft returning to Sawbridgeworth airfield at Allen's Green, 2 miles away. On public view are the names of rectors since 1327. 1594: Elizabeth I signed the appointment of the Revd Francis Burley, one of the translators of the King James Bible (1611). Six bells: oldest is the Number 6 dated 1628 with inscription 'God Save the King' (Charles I). In the churchyard is a yew tree 1,000 years old. *Tring*: St Peter and St Paul. One curate was James Austen, nephew of Jane Austen*. The fourteenth-century Tring tiles in the British Museum are part of a frieze taken from the church. They illustrate the childhood of Jesus in comic-strip style.

Churchill, Clementine (née Hozier) (1885–1977) Lived at 107 High Street, Berkhamsted*, and attended Bourne High School at No. 222. Took family laundry to a washerwoman near the Black Horse with her dog, which she trained to wipe its muddy paws on the mat. She was often invited back to her old school; the girls serenaded her with her most hated song, 'Clementine'. When she and Winston met they made each other laugh. A few days later she received an invitation to visit his mother, Jennie, at Salisbury Hall, from where Jennie later announced their engagement. After the honeymoon they returned there while looking for somewhere to live. She often booked into Dr Lief's Health Spa in Tring (Champneys*).

Churchill, Jennie (née Jerome) (1854–1921) The beautiful 'dollar princess' united her fortune to an English title. Dressed by Worth, wearing diamonds by Cartier, she married Lord Randolph, son of the Duke of Marlborough, at Blenheim Palace, where her son Winston was born seven months later. Randolph died of syphilis at 46. She scandalised her peers by marrying handsome, penniless George Cornwallis-West, at 25 the same age as her son Winston, when she was 45. Rented Salisbury Hall, a lovely Elizabethan moated mansion with grand staircase and oak-panelled rooms. She gave great parties at which her guests punted on the moat. Frequent guests included notorious friends, Alice Keppel (mistress of Edward VII) and Maxine Elliott. After her divorce, now aged 64, she again scandalised society when she married Montagu Porch, an Australian sheep farmer, who at 41 was younger than Winston. Tragic death: wearing high heels, she stumbled going downstairs and fell.

Churchill, John (1650–1722) 1st Duke of Marlborough. Son of the first Sir Winston. 1678: married Sarah Jennings*. 1685: James II elevated him to the peerage as Baron Churchill of Sandridge. 1703: created Duke of Marlborough. Holywell House, St Albans, was one of his homes.

Churchill, Randolph (1911–68) Son of Sir Winston. With wife Pamela, during the Second World War rented St Katherine's Rectory, Ickleford, just before the birth of Winston Jnr. A huge, eleven-bedroomed, ramshackle place so cold no rector had lived there since 1888, Pamela said of it: 'The house was very cold . . . I used to go to bed at 6.30 p.m. so as to turn off the gas fire.' The rectory, later bought by Martin Dent, the publisher, was demolished in the 1960s.

Churchill, Sir Winston (1874–1965) Statesman, war leader. Founded Special Operations Executive*. Proposed to Pamela Plowden, daughter of the Governor of Bengal, who rejected him in favour of Lord Lytton, Viceroy of India, but they remained firm friends and he was a frequent visitor to Knebworth*.

Civil War (1642–8) In the main, the county was Parliamentarian. The Parliamentarian Earl of Essex used St Albans as his head-quarters. Lands were confiscated from Royalists unless they could prove they supported Cromwell. That did not deter Sir Thomas Coningsby, Royalist Sheriff, from reading a public proclamation urging locals to support the King. After the war, soldiers, furious because they had not been paid, railed against Cromwell on Thriploe Heath, Royston*, and Corkbush Field, Ware*. After the Restoration, confiscated estates were restored to their owners.

Cobbett, William (1763–1835) First to record parliamentary debates (now Hansard). Often in prison convicted of sedition. Passionate about preserving rural self-sufficiency in an England gripped by agricultural and industrial revolution, in 1822, aged almost 60, he started his

Rural Rides. He was incensed at the way London 'swelled out to the distance of six or seven miles' into Hertfordshire and said it put him in a vile mood. In the book he wrote about Royston*, St Albans*, Tring*, Ware* and Watford*. He was furious with hat manufacturers for importing cheap plait instead of using locally grown wheat. He also resented being charged to use pot-holed turnpike roads and avoided them. He refused to drink tea, dismissing it as foreign, spurned potatoes as 'an Irish root' and ate Hertfordshire swedes instead.

Cockburn, Claud (1904–81) Founder of satirical magazine *Private Eye* with Richard Ingrams and Willie Rushton. Left-wing journalist. Lived in Berkhamsted, educated at the Collegiate School. Close friend of schoolmate Graham Greene. MI5 spent thirty years watching him but found nothing. Wrote for the *Daily Worker*, a communist newspaper. Foreign correspondent for *The Times* until he started his own newspaper, the *Week*. The government closed it down when he wrote against the war. Fought in the Spanish Civil War with George Orwell.

Colleges Bernard de Baliol (1135–67), Lord of the Manor of Hitchin, lived at Temple Dinsley*. His descendant John de Baliol (d. 1269) founded *Balliol College, Oxford*. De Clare, Lord of the Manor of Standon, fought with William I. His descendant Lady Elizabeth de Clare (Lady de Burgh), grand-daughter of Edward I, founded *Clare College, Cambridge*, in 1336. Sir Thomas Pope (1507–59) of Tyttenhanger* founded *Trinity College, Oxford*. Dr John Keys (1510–73), Lord of the Manors of Croxley and Cassiobury, refounded his old college Gonville Hall, Cambridge after which it became *Gonville and Caius*. John Colet of Wendover (1467–1519), Dean of St Paul's, founded

Effigy of Bernard de Baliol, St Mary's Church, Hitchin.

St Paul's School, London. John Eliot (1604–90) of Widford* founded *Harvard University* in America. Emily Davies (1830–1921) founded the UK's first women's college in Hitchin (later *Girton College, Cambridge*).

Comet May 1952: the Queen Mother and Princess Margaret flew in the world's first* jet aircraft, the de Havilland Comet. After touring the works and production line at Hatfield, they flew over France, Italy and the Swiss Alps before returning four hours later. The Queen Mother, who took the controls, sent a telegram from Hatfield to No. 600 (City of London) Squadron, of which she was Honorary Air Commodore: 'I am delighted to tell you that today I took over as pilot of a Comet aircraft. We exceeded a reading of 0.8 Mach at 40,000ft.'

Cooper, William (1813–85) Veterinarian. Invented world-famous sheep-dip. Dismissed as a quack when he started experimenting in his back yard, he ended up the largest employer in Berkhamsted for 100 years. Sheep scab was a serious problem for farmers until he developed his arsenic and sulphur dip. He built two factories and bought The Poplars. Some 120 employees accompanied his coffin to Berkhamsted Cemetery. 1911: Coopers granted Royal Warrant: Supplier of Sheep Dip to the Sovereign. 1959: Wellcome Laboratories bought the business but continued trading as Coopers. 1992: Wellcome sold out to Roussel.

Coprolite 1881 census shows 'fossil diggers'; they earned four times the wages of a farm labourer. Believed to be fossilised dinosaur dung, coprolite occurred in 12in layers 25ft below ground, and was used as fertiliser. Coprolite 'mines' survived at Ashwell and Pirton until 1901.

Cowper, William (1731–1800) Jane Austen's* favourite poet. Born and brought up in Berkhamsted*, where his father, chaplain to George II and nephew of Earl Cowper, was Rector of St Peter's. Memorial east window. Monument to his mother, Anne Donne, a relative of John Donne, in the Lady Chapel. The rectory, where he was born, was demolished. Remembered for the very funny 'John Gilpin's Ride' (a true story). After his mother died he was sent to live with friends in Aldbury, then to school in Markyate, where he was bullied. In and out of asylum in Lower Dagnall Street, St Albans: the Collegium Insanorum was founded by Nathaniel Cotton in 1760 and demolished in 1910. Wrote 'God Moves in a Mysterious Way' and 'Oh For a Closer Walk with God'.

Craig, Gordon (1872–1966) President of the Mermaid Theatre, London. Son of actress Ellen Terry*; lover of Isadora Duncan. Born at 18 Railway Street (now Orchard Street, Old Stevenage) and brought up in Harpenden, he married a girl from nearby Gustard Wood. He was the most avant-garde stage designer of his time. Stevenage New Town theatre named in his honour.

Cromer Post Mill Last windmill in the county. Open weekends from mid-May to mid-September. The first mill was built in about 1222. This one was built in 1681, closed around 1923 and restored in stages by the Hertfordshire Building Preservation Trust* 1967–98. Grinding is not possible but the sails turn in the wind. 1903: there were still working windmills at Albury, Anstey, Arkley, Bushey Heath, Great Hormead, Little Hadham, Tring and Weston.

Cromwell, Oliver (1599–1658) Regicide. Seized the High Sheriff of the county on his way to St Albans. The Parliamentarian army camped in Royston*, from where he sent his manifesto to the City of London authorities.

1645: headquarters at Sun Hotel, Hitchin, where 3,000 troops billeted. Camped at Royston before taking his army to St Albans two days before the Battle of Naseby. 13 November: based his HQ at Hertford Castle. 1647: soldiers at Royston refused to fight until Cromwell paid their wages. They marched to Baldock and Stevenage on their way to London to besiege parliament and were finally paid at St Albans.

Cromwell, Richard (1626–1712) Son of Oliver. Also Lord Protector until the Rump Parliament abolished the Protectorate on 7 May 1659. When Charles II was crowned, Cromwell left for Paris to escape creditors and those wanting his head. He, wife Dorothy Mayor (of Hursley, Hants) and son Oliver travelled under the name of Clarke. 1675: his wife died, possibly in Geneva.

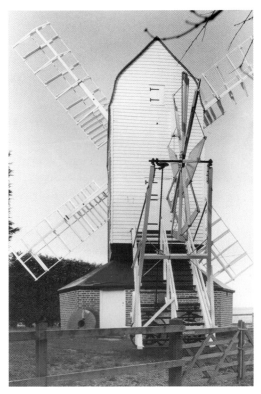

Cromer Post Mill.

1680: he returned to England. Some sources say he owned land in Hertfordshire. He paid 10s a week for lodgings with Sergeant and Mrs Pengelly in the Old Parsonage, Cheshunt. Churchgate is on the site of the house, which burnt down in 1888. Local legend says he dressed like a poor farmer and saw Queen Anne on the throne he once graced. His son died in 1705. Richard moved to Hursley, where he lived as lord of the manor. He is buried inside the church.

Croxley Green Croc = one who makes coins (for Canute in 1016). Domesday Book: 'Croc's Lea'. Famous for superior quality watermarked notepaper. Croxley Hall Farm has a huge barn, the second largest in England. Built c. 1400 for the abbots of St Albans. 1975: sympathetically restored by the County Council but still in need of a lot of work. Dubbed 'Wolsey's slaughterhouse', it supplied the Cardinal's gargantuan feasts at nearby Moor Park*. The farm was once the manor house belonging to Dr John Keys (1510–73), physician to Edward VI and Mary Tudor. 1588: he bought the manors of Croxley and Cassiobridge from the Crown for £23 to refound his old college, Gonville Hall, Cambridge, after which it became known as *Gonville and Caius*. 1829: John Dickinson started producing machine-made paper. 1980: his mill closed after 150 years, leaving 900 unemployed. 1925: when the Metropolitan Railway reached here, the developers moved in and never left. This is part of Betjeman's* beloved Metroland. Stone's Community Orchard is a relic of one four times as large where Cherry Sundays were held in July. Hertfordshire black cherries, as well as local apple varieties and plums, are among the still-flowering trees that Walter Stone may have planted. Barbara Woodhouse (1910–88), famous dog trainer, lived here. Her BBC series *Training Dogs The Woodhouse Way* is now cult TV. The eccentric, bossy senior citizen in kilt and sensible shoes was a former horse trainer who developed forceful techniques for teaching dogs and their owners obedience.

Cunningham, John (1917–2002) Group Captain, Wing Commander, DSO, DFC.

Group Captain John 'Cat's Eyes' Cunningham with de Havilland 'Moth', the eighth built and the oldest aircraft on the British Civil Register. Woburn, 1988.

War hero. 1935: joined de Havilland Technical School as an apprentice. 1941: Hunsdon* 85 Squadron. He was the most famous night-fighter of the war during the Battle of Britain blitz on London; nickname 'Cat's Eyes' Cunningham. His was the first plane to have radar, so secret few knew of it, especially not Goering, until it was too late. 1946: chief test pilot for de Havilland. Helped develop the Comet, Britain's first jet airliner, setting an international flight record in the aircraft on 16 October 1957. He also helped to set up Britain's first aircraft museum at Salisbury Hall*.

Curiosities aka Peculiars. Hertfordshire Puddingstone*. The Hertfordshire Spike*. Ashwell* church graffiti recording the Black Death. Ayot St Lawrence* New Church, a strange Palladian edifice. Bedmond: the English Pope. Berkhamsted* bookstall: buyers put money through a hole in the wall to the tune of £1,000 every year. Boxmoor*: black and white striped cattle. Codicote: thatched silo. Coleman Green*: chimney in the middle of a field. Hitchin*: the British School*. Letchworth*: black squirrels*; first* roundabout. Old Stevenage: Henry Trigg is on the rafters of a barn (or is he?). Radlett: highest proportion of Jewish residents in the UK (24.1 per cent). Royston Cave. Sarratt* church: saddleback roof. Tring: fleas in Victorian clothes and *glis glis**. Villages: Nasty and Cold Christmas (Greenwich Meridian 0° longitude passes through). Ware*: Gazebos, the Great Bed, the Grotto. Winkwell: mechanised swing bridge.

D

Deer The red deer or hart, Britain's largest land mammal, is the county's symbol. Where can we see it? According to an Ashridge spokesman, we can't. Red deer are privately owned, as often as not in royal parks. 1989: the magnificent sculptures by Stephen Elson were put up outside County Hall, Hertford. Almost 7ft high, one is standing, the other is bowed. We can see fallow deer on the Ashridge Estate, 900 of them. Half a million visitors every year do. Females have a fawn every year but this has to be balanced against 100 deer killed each year in road accidents.

Deer Parks (selection) Ardeley Bury (1220), Bayfordbury (1766), Bedwell (pre-1406), Broadfield Hall (medieval), Golden Parsonage (medieval), King's Walden Bury (1695), Offley Place (1676), Pishiobury (1343), The Bury, Sacombe Park (1676).

Defoe, Daniel (1660–1731) Writer. When social historians research life in England they turn to Cobbett*, Defoe*, Evelyn*, Fiennes*, and Pepys*. One of the reasons for his *Tour through the Whole Island of Great Britain* at the age of 64 was, it is thought, to gather intelligence. In the book he mentions Baldock*, Barley*, Bushey*, Cassiobury*, Hatfield*, Hemel*, Hitchin*, St Albans*, South Mimms, Royston*, Tring* and Ware*.

de Havilland, Sir Geoffrey (1882–1965) CBE. Aircraft designer. Pilot in the First World War. One of the most famous names in the history of British aviation. Conceived the DH106 Comet (first* jet

The Hart, symbol of the county, sculpted by Stephen Elson.

Statue of Sir Geoffrey de Havilland, designed by Keith Maddison in 1997, stands at the entrance to the University of Hertfordshire.

De Havilland Comet Racer *Grosvenor House* (1934) and a de Havilland Comet airliner (1959) together at Hatfield, 1992.

airliner) and the Trident (first tri-jet airliner). 1930: moved to Hatfield. 1931: DH82 Tiger Moth. 1934: DH88 Comet Racer won England to Australia air race (model outside Comet Hotel, Hatfield). His offer to build a 230-mph racer so that Britain could enter the competition was advertised. Three were ordered: by Jim and Amy Mollison (née Johnson*), racing driver Bernard Rubins and A.O. Edwards MD, Grosvenor House Hotel. The Mollisons' plane was black and gold, Rubins's green; the other, red and white and named Grosvenor House, won. 1940: Mosquito unarmed bomber (faster than the Spitfire). 1944: second son John killed on a Mosquito test flight. 1946: eldest son Geoffrey died in the DH108 practising for world speed record attempt; buried with his brother in Tewin churchyard. The boys' mother died shortly afterwards.

1949: DH106 Comet, the world's first jet-powered passenger aircraft. 1950s: DH Propeller Co. built Blue Streak*. 1960: company taken over by Hawker Siddeley. The famous DH logo disappeared. 1965: Sir Geoffrey died at Watford Peace Memorial Hospital. He is buried with his wife and sons. His statue is outside the University of Hertfordshire, Hatfield.

Democracy First* began in Hertfordshire in 1213 (only for rich people) when a council was held at St Albans to discuss King John's* misrule. It drafted Magna Carta. 1295: the Model Parliament met at St Albans under Edward I. Every city, town and borough sent two representatives. Topic for debate: 'What touches all should be approved by all.'

Dickens, Charles (1812–70) Novelist. Travelled all over the county as a young

Charles Dickens as a young reporter.

newspaper reporter. 1835: first visit when he was 23, working for the *Morning Chronicle*, to report on the fire at Hatfield House in which the west wing was gutted and the fox-hunting Marchioness of Salisbury died. After Bill Sykes murdered Nancy (*Oliver Twist*), he hid in Eight Bells in Fore Street. When rumbled, he left Hatfield for St Albans. In *Christmas Stories* Mrs Lirriper spent her honeymoon at the Salisbury Arms in Fore Street. When Mr Lirriper died, Dickens buried him in Hatfield churchyard. Close friend of Edward Bulwer-Lytton*, after whom he named one of his many sons (Edward Bulwer Lytton Dickens is buried in Australia). Often stayed at Knebworth*. Visited Lucas* the hermit at nearby Redcoats Farm. 1824: he retold the murder of William Weare in *Sketches of Gentlemen* and *Martin Chuzzlewit* (the Elstree

murder*). With Lytton he formed the Guild of Literature and built houses in Stevenage for impoverished writers, but they refused to leave London.

Dickens, Monica (1915–92) Great-granddaughter of Charles Dickens. Published wartime experiences: *One Pair of Hands* about being a char and *One Pair of Feet* about being a nurse. 1946: moved to Hinxworth, which she loved, and took a job on the local paper. Wrote column for *Woman's Own*. *Flowers on the Grass*, *Angel in the Corner* and *My Turn to Make the Tea* are about her time here. She helped run the local cricket team and became a parish councillor and treasurer of Ashwell Horse Show. 1951: she met and married a US naval officer, moved to America and adopted two girls. 1985: her husband died and she returned to England.

Dickinson, John (1782–1869) Paper mills ran for 200 years. Famous brand names of Croxley Script, Colne Valley Parchment and Lion. Before his time paper was hand-made in sheets. 1807: Dickinson patented machine to make paper in rolls. Perforated metal cylinders with tight wire mesh covers revolved inside a vat of pulp. The water was drained and fibres on the surface were carried off by an endless web of felt passing through a roller. Mills: Apsley, Batchworth, Home Park and Nash. He built cottages for his workers at Croxley Green* (Dickinson Square conservation area). 1829: patented a process for running silk thread through paper (used in banknotes). 1980: mill closed.

Digswell Once called High Welwyn. Inside the old church are brasses of Sir John Peryent (d. 1432) and his wife, Lady Joan (d. 1415). Sir John was pennon-bearer (royal lance with swallow-tail streamer) to Richard II and Master of Horse to Joan of Navarre, second wife of Henry IV. His wife was her

Digswell Viaduct, Welwyn.

chief lady-in-waiting. Frank Wells (1903–82), son of H.G. Wells, lived in Mill House (he died in Welwyn). In the 1930s he co-directed silent films with his father. All starred Elsa Lanchester. By the time they were released, talkies had arrived and Angle Pictures folded. Both Peryent and Wells fade into insignificance beside the magnificent viaduct. Grade II listed, 1,560ft long, it passes over the Mimram Valley 98ft above the river. It has 40 × 30ft-span arches and was designed by Cubitt, chief engineer to the Great Northern Railway, to resemble a Roman aqueduct. It took a mere two years to build with bricks said to have been made on site, where the workmen lived. 8 August 1850: the first train from London to Peterborough crossed. Passengers look down on 17 acres of lake, wood and parkland. Local legend has it Queen Victoria* refused to cross. Today it carries the King's Cross to Edinburgh train. There is talk of making the line four (instead of two) tracks, which would mean building a second viaduct. It is estimated that in its lifetime it has carried more traffic than any other viaduct or bridge in the world.

Du Maurier, Sylvia and Trixie Daughters of George (Trilby) du Maurier, as young mothers lived near each other in Berkhamsted*. When Trixie married Charlie Millar, a city merchant, they moved there to raise a family. Their first of four sons died as a baby and is buried in Berkhamsted. Trixie died young and is buried next to him. Sylvia married Arthur Llewellyn Davies, barrister. His aunt Emily Davies founded Girton* College in Hitchin. When Arthur died, Sylvia, with five sons and no income, became unhinged, so J.M. Barrie* became their legal guardian. Their brother Gerald, inspiration for du Maurier cigarettes, acted in Barrie plays and was the first Captain Hook. He and his family spent summers at Croxley Green*. His daughter was the novelist Daphne. As children the du Mauriers had a St Bernard dog, which was portrayed in *Peter Pan*.

Duke of St Albans One of Britain's twenty-four dukes. Son of Charles II and Nell Gwyn, his favourite mistress from 1668 till his death in 1684 ('Let not poor Nelly starve' was his deathbed wish), the first* duke was Charles Beauclerk (1670–1726), born in Lincoln's Inn Fields. Coat of arms has a baton sinister, meaning he was a natural (illegitimate) son of the king but not a legitimate heir to the throne. The myth that Nell dangled him out of a window of Salisbury Hall until Charles II conferred a title on him is simply that. He did not become Duke of St Albans until he was 14. 1694: when he married Lady Diana de Vere, daughter of the Earl of Oxford, he was given an annual pension from the Crown of £2,000. His post as hereditary Grand Falconer of England, granted by his father, brought in an extra £1,500 p.a. 1703: the Parliament of Ireland granted him £800 p.a. for publicly condemning the anti-Catholic Sacheverell Riots. 1718: made a Knight of the Garter. 1953: the 12th Duke, as Master Falconer, refused to attend the Queen's coronation when told he could not take a live falcon to the ceremony, only a stuffed one. The 13th Duke, a salesman, when sued for unpaid income tax, left the country. The 14th Duke is a chartered accountant. The only visit of any of the dukes to the eponymous town was in the 1970s.

E

Easter The pagan goddess 'Eostre' was worshipped in spring to celebrate the resurrection of the earth after winter. The decision to celebrate that of Jesus at the same time was a clever move by early Christians. To make sure it became a Christian tradition, in 673 the Church in England held its first* Synod* at Hertford. All five English bishops attended to settle the abiding question: when is Easter Sunday? The Synod decided it should be the first Sunday following the first full moon after 21 March. It took 1,200 years to commemorate the event with a stone outside Hertford Castle.

Edgar Atheling (1052–1126) Raised by Edward the Confessor and nominated his heir, he is known as the lost king of England. Son of Edward the Exiled (by Canute), grandson of Edmund Ironside, he was proclaimed king by the Witan following the death of King Harold at Hastings in 1066. Thirteen years old – too young to fight the invasion – he was never crowned and submitted to William the Conqueror. William treated Edgar well until Estridson, King of Denmark and nephew of Canute, who said Edgar was the rightful king, invaded England in 1069. When the Danes captured York, William paid them to leave. Edgar escaped to Scotland until his niece Edith, aka Matilda, married Henry I in 1100, and he was allowed to return to his estates in Hertfordshire.

Edgeworth, Maria (1768–1849) Novelist. Family owned Edgeware, then called Edge-worth. Her most famous book was *Castle Rackrent*, based on the true story of Lady Cathcart*. Maria lived between Gossoms End and Northchurch from the age of 9 until she left school and the family went to Ireland. She admired Jane Austen* and wrote to her with helpful hints(!). Austen, in return, admired her writing (*Northanger Abbey* reflects aspects of *Castle Rackrent*). Maria often stayed with Sir John Sebright* in Beechwood and Lady Salisbury at Hatfield. She also visited Peter* the Wild Boy and tried to teach him to talk.

Edmund of Hadham aka Edmund Tudor* (1430–56), Earl of Richmond, father of Henry VII.

Edmund of Langley (1341–1402) Prince. Fifth son of Edward III and Phillippa of Hainault, brother of the Black Prince, first Duke of York. Born King's Langley. Married Isabella of Castile. His great-grandson was the usurper Edward IV. 1965: Edmund and Isabella's tomb in All Saints' Church, King's

The tomb of Edmund of Langley, All Saints' Church, King's Langley.

Langley, was visited by Enoch Powell MP. After studying the Royal Coats of Arms, he said they were not those of Edmund and Isabella, but of Richard II and his wife Anne of Bohemia. When Anne died in 1394, a heartbroken Richard II* abandoned the tomb. Just as well. He would never have been put in it, as he was starved to death in Pontefract Castle and buried in secret.

Edward, the Black Prince (1330–76) An almost king. First son of Edward III, Prince of Wales, he was known as the Black Prince because he wore black armour at the Battle of Crécy. Sometimes referred to as Edward IV because he was England's guardian when his father was out of the country. He and Joan, the fair maid of Kent, honeymooned at Berkhamsted Castle, his main and favourite home. The Arms of Berkhamsted have a castle with three towers with a border from the Arms of the Duchy of Cornwall. 1367: King and Queen at St Albans said goodbye before the Prince went into battle. The crown passed to the next in line, his son Richard II*.

Edward (1453–71) Another almost king. Prince of Wales, son of Henry VI*. Was present at the Second Battle of St Albans. At Tewkesbury, on the order of Edward IV, the usurper, he was publicly humiliated before being slaughtered.

Edward the Confessor (d. 1066) Based his Royal Mint at Hart Ford.

Edward I (1239–1307) Married La Infanta de Castile, the beloved Eleanor* of all the crosses. To placate the Welsh for the killing of the Prince of Wales he gave them a new one, his son Edward II, born in Wales and known there as Edward of Caernarfon. Since then the male heir to the throne has always been named Prince of Wales. 1276: modernised King's Langley palace, his and Eleanor's much-loved favourite royal

residence. Some 500 oak trees on the estate were felled to rebuild the Tower of London. 1289: Eleanor died. Grief-stricken, Edward went to Ashridge to summon parliament. 1295: parliament summoned to St Albans. 1299: remarried, taking new wife Margaret of France to Langley and giving her Hertford Castle as a wedding gift. 1302: gave Langley to his son Edward (II) but exiled his lover, Frenchman Piers Gaveston.

Edward II (1284–1327) First English Prince of Wales. This is the Edward who married Isabella, 'She Wolf of France'*. 1307: Edward crowned. His lover Piers Gaveston returned from exile to marry Margaret de Clare at Berkhamsted Castle. Edward attended the wedding and, wanting Piers near, gave him the castle as a wedding present and created him Earl of Cornwall. 1308: Edward left England to marry Isabella in Boulogne, leaving Piers in charge of his kingdom. Isabella was the sister of Charles IV of France. 1309: Knights Templar* arrested at Temple Dinsley* on Edward's order. Edward and Piers spent Christmas at Langley. 1312: Piers murdered by the barons, who forced Edward to produce an heir. The future Edward III was born nine months later. 1315: Edward gave Piers an elaborate funeral at Langley. His embalmed body was brought from Oxford and reinterred in the Friary church. The Archbishop of St Albans was asked to conduct the ceremony, and in return was given a huge sum of money for the abbey. A carved portrait on Edward is on one of the stone corbels inside. He was murdered in Berkeley Castle.

Edward III (1312–77) Like his father and grandfather he loved Langley and was often there with his wife, Philippa of Hainault. 1328: Edward and Philippa, on a Royal Progress, stopped at Hitchin. 1330: Edward placed his mother, aged 36, in 'honourable confinement' at Hertford Castle but visited her often. 1337: created his son Edward, Prince of Wales, 1st Duke of Cornwall and gave him Berkhamsted Castle (still owned by the Duchy). 1341: fifth son, Edmund*, born at Langley. 1347: the Black Death. The court took up residence at Langley. 1358: Isabella died at Hertford Castle. Edward paid guards to protect her corpse until she was buried. Gave Hertford Castle to his son John of Gaunt.

Edward IV (1461–83) Usurper. Proclaimed himself king in 1461. 1468: fell in love with Elizabeth Woodville, widow of Sir John Grey (killed in the Second Battle* of St Albans). An older woman, she refused to become his mistress and so he married her and gave her Hertford Castle as a wedding present. 1465: Elizabeth held court at Hertford Castle. 1469: Edward gave Berkhamsted Castle and King's Langley to his mother, Cicely. 1789: when new paving stones were laid in St George's Chapel, Windsor, the vault of Edward IV was discovered. His tomb was opened in the presence of Horace Walpole, and several people cut off locks of his hair. One, somehow, found its way into Hoddesdon Museum.

Edward VI (1537–53) As a child he lived at Hatfield, Hunsdon and Hertford Castle, where he died. He gave Hertford to Princess Mary and Hunsdon to Princess Elizabeth.

Eleanor Crosses Eleanor of Castile was 10 when she married Edward I, a love match. They had sixteen children. 1289: Edward left for Scotland and asked Eleanor to join him. On the way she was taken ill and died in Harby, Nottinghamshire. Devastated, Edward ordered a memorial cross to be built in each of the twelve places where her corpse rested overnight on its journey back to London. Only three, those at Geddington

Eleanor Cross at Waltham: one of three (out of twelve) remaining in England.

and Hardingstone in Northamptonshire and Waltham (cost £92) in Hertfordshire, survive. Cromwell's soldiers shot at the other Hertfordshire cross, in St Albans; it was demolished in 1702 and replaced by the present clock tower.

Eliot, George (1819–80) Novelist. 17 June 1875: one of the most famous writers in the world arrived in Rickmansworth. George Eliot was a pseudonym of Mrs Marian Lewes, but her name was neither Marian nor Lewes, it was Mary Cross. Her home was in London, but halfway through *Daniel Deronda* (her last novel, although she was not to know it) the builders arrived. A friend suggested she rent The Elms and not go home until the work was finished. The book

The Elms, Rickmansworth, where George Eliot wrote part of her last novel, *Daniel Deronda*. It is now Joan of Arc School.

she was writing was about Jews. A rabbi friend dreamed of a Jewish national home in Palestine, so she let Daniel Deronda establish it. The BBC spent £6 million filming the story. The Elms is now Joan of Arc School. Outside is a statue of St Joan unveiled in 1939 by the French Ambassador to Britain.

Elizabeth I (1533–1603) Knew the county well and loved it. 1538: a virtual prisoner with half-sister Mary at Hatfield. 1543: with Mary and Edward at Ashridge. 1553: imprisoned at Ashridge. 1554: Mary ordered her to attend court to answer charges of treason. Unwell, she stopped off at Redbourn, St Albans and Mymms. Imprisoned at Hatfield. 1558: at Hatfield when told she was Queen. 1561: stayed with Sir Ralph Sadleir at Standon before moving on to Hertford Castle. Her visit cost him £1,920. 1564: stayed with William Cecil at Theobalds. 1570: stayed with Sir Nicholas Bacon, Lord Keeper of the Great Seal, in his little house at Gorhambury. 1571: stayed at Hunsdon with 'dear coz' Henry Carey. 1575: stayed at Gorhambury for fourteen days before moving on to Theobalds to stay with Lord Burghley. One night cost him £332. 1577: visit to Gorhambury cost Sir Nicholas Bacon £577 for four days. 1578: stayed at Much Hadham Hall. 1583: stayed at Theobalds. 1586: appointed love of her life Robert Dudley Lord Lieutenant of Hertfordshire and gave him Boxmoor. July 1588: Spanish Armada sighted. Beacons lit at Amwell, Gravely, Monken Hadley and

St Albans. Sir William Lytton of Knebworth gathered forces in the county and led them to Tilbury where Lord Hunsdon was in command. 1591: ten days at Theobalds cost her host £1,000.

Elizabeth II (b. 1926) 1952: a new Queen opened a New Town, Hemel Hempstead 20 April 1959: opened the Royal Veterinary Training College*, North Mymms, lunched with uncle David (mother's brother) at St Paul's Walden before opening Queensway, Stevenage, the first* car-free shopping centre in Britain. To commemorate her visit she unveiled a panel on the clock tower in Town Square.

Elizabeth, the Queen Mother (1900–2002) Elizabeth Bowes-Lyon, youngest daughter of Claude Bowes-Lyon, Earl of Strathmore, Lord Glamis. Born 4 August 1900, ninth of ten children; her father did not register her birth within the statutory six weeks and so was fined 7s 6d. When he did, he recorded that she had been born in St Paul's Waldenbury*, but it was in fact at St Thomas Hospital, London. She was baptised at St Paul's Walden, where she was brought up, and visited there every July. 1904–13: her tutor was Marion Wilkie of Dacre Road, Hitchin, who cycled to The Bury every day until her health gave out. After that Elizabeth and her younger brother David were driven to her in a pony and trap. They also had dancing lessons in the ballroom of the Sun Hotel, Hitchin. 1923: Elizabeth accepted marriage proposal from Prince Albert, Duke of York, at The Bury. They often visited The Bury as a family. 1952: first of the royals to fly in the de Havilland Comet*. 14 July 1956: laid foundation stone for St George's, Stevenage, the largest Anglican church (Coventry is a cathedral) built in Britain since the war. 27 November 1960: she returned for the consecration and gave the church a rare and valuable George III communion plate. The church became the Church of St George and St Andrew in 1984 following the closure of St Andrew's, Bedwell Crescent. 1963: opened the QEII Hospital on one of her many visits 'home'.

Elstree Film Studios Borehamwood*. In 1914, when it was no longer possible to film in London because of pea-souper fogs caused by pollution, the Neptune Film Company opened here. 1926: purpose-built state-of-the-art studios (still in use). *Indiana Jones*, *Raiders of the Lost Ark*, *Star Wars*, *James Bond*, *2001 A Space Odyssey*, *Saving Private Ryan* and *Sleepy Hollow* all made here. George Lucas, Steven Spielberg and Stanley Kubrick filmed here. Home of TV's *Big Brother*, *Who Wants to be a Millionaire?*, *Eastenders*, *Casualty* and *Top of the Pops* among much else.

Elstree Murder Just as Elstree studios are not in Elstree, the murder did not happen here, but in Radlett*. The body of William Weare was found here – hence newspaper headlines 'The Elstree Murder' – and buried in St Nicholas's churchyard. Also buried here is Martha Ray, mistress of John Montagu, Earl of Sandwich, inventor of the sandwich and patron of Captain Cook. He and 17-year-old Martha lived at his mansion in Hinchingbrooke as husband and wife for seventeen years and had five children. In 1779 the Revd Mr Hackman, who was obsessed with her, shot Martha at Covent Garden Opera House.

English Heritage Has the authority to register any site of Special Historic Interest. Although the following are privately owned, if an application for development might affect them, local authorities must consult English Heritage: Aldenham House; Amwell Grove and Pool; Ashridge; Ashwell Bury;

Ayot House; Balls Park; Bayfordbury; Benington Lordship; Berkhamsted Castle; Broadway, Letchworth; Brocket Hall; Cassiobury Park; Cokenach; Fanhams Hall; Garden House, Cottered; Gobions; Goldings; Gorhambury; Hatfield House; Hexton Manor; Homewood, Knebworth; Howard Park, Letchworth; Julians, Rushden; Moor Park; Napsbury Hospital, St Albans; Panshanger; Pishiobury; Poles Park; Roman Wall, St Albans; Rothamsted Manor, Harpenden; Scott's Grotto, Ware; St Paul's Walden; Temple Dinsley; Tewin Water; Tring Park; Woodhall Park; Wrotham Park; Youngsbury.

Enigma Code-breaking machine. When Alan Turing designed the 'bombe' for the machine, Commander Travis took the drawings to the chief engineer of the British Tabulating Machine Company, Icknield Way, Letchworth*. It took five weeks to make the first machine (dubbed Agnes), and it was delivered to Bletchley Park in 1940. After that each black iron monster, with dimensions 8 × 12 × 3ft, took a week to build. The name 'bombe' was dreamed up by the Poles because it resembled their round ice cream, called a bomba.

Essendon Guide books mention Cuffley as the place where the Zeppelin* airship was brought down, but forget to say that on its way it bombed St Mary's Church here. 1778: Mary Whitbread presented a black basalt Wedgwood font to the church (too valuable to be on show). Bedwell Park was the home of Sam Whitbread, the brewer. His son Sam (1764–1815), a politician, bought nearby Woolmers. A social reformer whose ideas came to fruition after his suicide (e.g. the Poor Law Bill), he empathised with Caroline, Princess of Wales, the betrayed wife of George IV, and championed her cause in the House of Commons. Camfield Place was the home of Beatrix Potter's* grandparents and later of Dame Barbara Cartland*. In 1892, when her grandmother was dying, Beatrix Potter stayed at Bedwell Park.

Esterhazy, Walsin Ferdinand (1847–1923) Spy, traitor. Following his exposure during the Dreyfus affair in France (1894), he hid in Harpenden, where he eventually died. He lived as Count Villemont, but MI5 knew who he was.

Evacuees The Second World War saw the largest migration in British history. Four million children were evacuated from the cities to the countryside or overseas. Air raids in London in September 1940 meant the county's population grew by 150,000 in a matter of weeks (10,000 in Hemel Hempstead alone).

Evelyn, John (1620–1706) His famous diaries were published in 1818. Wrote about Hatfield House*, the Harrisons' new house Balls Park, Hertingfordbury Park, Theobalds and St Albans. 1666: spent four days at Cassiobury with his friend the Earl of Essex. 1685: accompanied the Lord Lieutenant of Hertfordshire to St Albans. 1692: riding with officers taking tax revenues from Hertfordshire to London, they were ambushed by men who tied them up and shot the horses so they could not follow them.

F

Faldo, Nick (b. 1957) Golfer. MBE. First Briton in fifty-four years to win three British Opens, only player after Jack Nicklaus to win two successive US Masters, one of only seven to win the Masters and British Open in one year. First player (1992) to earn £1 million in one season. Born in Welwyn Garden City, he took lessons at the local club and within two years was an accomplished golfer. The course ran alongside the Great North Road, onto which balls were frequently hit, and was altered when the A1(M) was built. 1975: played in schoolboy international alongside Sandy Lyle and Ian Woosnam. 1976: won British Youths Open Amateur Championship, English Amateur Championship and Berkshire Trophy. 1977: turned professional. 2002: Nick Faldo Golf Institute opened at Brocket Hall to teach the Faldo way. 'Brocket Hall . . . two miles from where I was born enables me to put something positive back into the area which I have a deep affection for . . . bursaries to enable underprivileged youngsters develop their skills.'

Fanshawe, Anne (1625–80) Feisty wife of a diplomat. Always travelled with him. Brought up at Balls Park*, the estate of her father Sir John Harrison. Many of her children are buried nearby with her parents and husband. Her Royalist family was bankrupted by Cromwell, as was that of her husband, Sir Richard Fanshawe of Ware Park, diplomat to Charles II.

Ferrers, Lady Katherine (1634–60) 'Near the cell, there is a well, Near the well there is a tree, And under the tree the treasure be.' The 'cell' refers to Markyate Cell, an old monastery near Wheathampstead. This is a local rhyme regarding the supposed whereabouts of supposed treasure stolen by the supposed 'Wicked Lady'. There is nothing to connect her with highway robbery and she may have been confused with 'Wicked Lord Ferrers' (no relation), hanged in 1760. An heiress at the age of 6, she was made a ward of court by Richard Fanshawe*, who married her against her will at age 14 to 16-year-old Thomas Fanshawe. The Fanshawes sold Markyate Cell in 1655, five years before she died and it is thought the legend was dreamed up in 1820 following the discovery there of a secret room. She was buried at St Mary's, Ware, June 1660, it is said by night and in secret, in unconsecrated ground outside the family tomb. If true – as that meant she would not

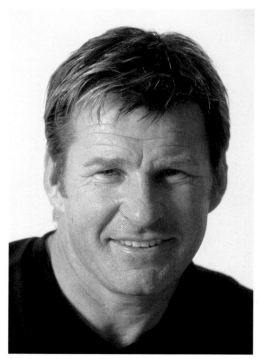

Nick Faldo.

go to heaven but to another place – one must ask why.

Fiennes, Celia (1662–1741) Diarist. Rode side-saddle through every county in England. She travelled out of curiosity between the ages of 20 and 35. 1697: on her 'Northern Journey' she visited Broxbourne*, Haileybury* and 'Amwell', where nieces Susanna and Mary Filmer joined her. Thomas Filmer was a London lawyer who owned Amwellbury. They travelled on to Ware*, Wareside, Baker's End, Much Hadham* and Bishop's Stortford. Signposts were 6ft above the ground for the convenience of riders, but she complained that latches on gates were so low that she had to dismount to open them. She also objected to paying tolls.

Film 1912: Borehamwood Studios. 1914: Welwyn Studios. 1926: Elstree Studios. Film companies have a choice of 4,000 locations in the county, earn £50 million p.a. for the county and provide 7 per cent of employment in 2,500 film-related companies. *Harry Potter* alone provided 1,700 jobs. Millions of film-goers the world over see the county listed in credits. Hertfordshire International Film Festival (HIFF), an annual showcase for independent cinema, premieres award-winning shorts and films from around the world.

Firsts (selection). *In the world*: democracy, English pope, Garden City, jet plane, medical textbook in English, New Town, Quaker Meeting House (purpose built), translators (into English) of Homer and Aesop. *In Britain*: aircraft museum, BBC regional transmitter, Christian martyr, church by Gilbert Scott*, English GP to royalty, Halifax flight, health farm, Norman castle, naturist camp, mail-order packet of seeds, paper, paper-making machine, car-free town centre, roundabout, Church Synod, talkie, women's college, woman sports writer.

Flaunden, the first church designed by Sir George Gilbert Scott.

Flaunden Pronounced 'Flarnden'. The village that moved. Today, 300ft above sea level, it is 2 miles from the old one. The original church, built in 1235 by Thomas Flaunden, was dedicated to St Mary Magdalene. Parishioners often arrived to find it flooded by the River Chess. It was abandoned when a new one was built on the hill in 1837, the first* church designed by Sir George Gilbert Scott. It was built for his uncle, vicar of nearby Latimer. Nothing remains of the old one. The Green Dragon pub was, so it is said, frequented by the Nazi von Ribbentrop, who was executed, and by the spy Guy Burgess, who was not.

Stratton's Folly.

Follies Folie = serving no purpose. 1700: Folly Arch, Brookmans Park: Sir Jeremy Sandbrooks built a great arch with castellated towers opening onto an avenue which led nowhere. 1789: Stratton's Folly, Little Berkhamsted: 100ft-high tower built by retired Admiral John Stratton so that he could see ships on the Thames. Impossible now, impossible then. 1830: George Proctor of Benington built an instant ruin (gate with castellated towers, portcullis and a faux moat). 1927: Carl Holmes, an American millionaire, opened a dairy farm at Codicote (The Node). He was so enamoured with old world England that he thatched the dung conveyor and silo.

Folly Island is in the middle of landlocked Hertford. Not always a folly, once a major link to the Port of London.

Football The England team trains at London Colney, where Arsenal has owned the ground for thirty years.

Forster, E.M. (1879–1970) 1883: his widowed mother rented Rooks Nest in (old) Stevenage when Morgan was 4. 1893: owner refused to renew the lease and they moved to Kent. *Howard's End*, a homage to Rooks Nest, is considered his masterpiece. 1945: his mother died. Forster contemplated moving back to Stevenage but was appalled by the plan to build 60,000 houses and turn Stevenage into Britain's first* New Town. He spoke about his horror on BBC radio and settled in Cambridge instead. The area where he lived has now been saved for posterity by people power*, the Friends of Forster Country.

Foundling Hospital Berkhamsted (Ashlyns School). By 1930, London was so unhealthy that the Thomas Coram Foundling Hospital built a school here. Children in uniform went everywhere in crocodiles, two by two. Every year the children went to their own holiday camp near Folkestone, and accompanied by the school band, marched from the school to the station to board a special train. Children were adopted by the organisation and given new names. Early records show Julius Caesars, William Shakespeares and Thomas Corams. In the Thomas Coram Museum, London, there is a photograph of boys marching out of the school for the last time on their way to Berkhamsted.

Fox, George (1624–91) Founder of the Quakers. Established Friends' Meeting Houses at Baldock, Barnet, Bishop's Stortford, Hertford, Markyate, St Albans. Spent the last six summers of his life in the county. The George and Dragon, Baldock, was dubbed the Quakers' Hostel. A close friend of William Penn*, with whom he took the Friends to America. Fox's Chair is in the first* purpose-built Friends' Meeting House, Railway Street, Hertford.

G

Gaddesden From the Gade. John Snr gave the Manor to Ashridge* College in 1283. John Jnr (1280–1361) was the first* Englishman appointed court physician (to Edward I*, Edward II* and Edward III*) so was the most famous doctor in England. In 1314 he wrote *Rosa Medicinae*, the first standard medical textbook in English. It was not published until 1492. He discovered desalination and distillation and said that urine can tell a doctor everything he needs to know about a patient's health. Died aged 81, when the average age of mortality was 30. Said to be a friend of Chaucer and the model for the Doctor of Physick in the Prologue to the *Canterbury Tales*. The black-and-white timber-framed house with overhanging storey, fifteenth-century hall and a roof of open timbers on the corner of Church Road bears the name John of Gaddesden. Parts date from John Jnr's time.

Garden Cities First* in the world was Letchworth* (1903). Next intended was Knebworth (1908). The First World War put paid to that. Welwyn came in 1919. Often wrongly referred to as New Towns*. The concept of a Garden City was pre-First World War, that of New Towns is post-Second World War.

Garden Designers: *Charles Bridgeman* (d. 1738): Royal Gardener: The Serpentine, Hyde Park; Round Pond, Kensington Gardens; in Hertfordshire: Briggens, Brocket, Cassiobury, Gobions, Moor Park, Sacombe and Tring Manor. *Lancelot 'Capability' Brown* (1715–83): Royal Gardener. Designs partially survive at Ashridge, Beechwood in Flamstead, Cole Green, Digswell, Gilston Park, Moor Park, Pishiobury and Youngsbury. *Gertrude Jekyll* (1843–1932): At 50, when her eyesight became too bad for painting, turned her attention to gardens (designed 300). She loved Sir Edwin Lutyens*, half her age. He loved her back and called her 'Bumps'. They were inseparable. She designed the garden at Temple Dinsley* (Princess Helena College) to complement the Lutyens' house extension. Knebworth House has a Jekyll herb garden (designed 1907, planted 1982). Remnants of her gardens at Ashwell Bury. Her original plans for the Muriel Wood (second wife of Sir Henry Wood) garden, Chorleywood are in the Museum of Garden History. Other designs include Amersfoot, Berkhamsted, Digswell Place, Hill End, Hitchin, Homewood, Knebworth and Fairhill. *Sir Geoffrey Jellicoe* (1900–96): Royal Gardener (Royal Lodge, Windsor Great Park). Designed the Water Garden, Hemel Hempstead, one of his favourite projects. Bridges take visitors from car parks to the centre. This is one of only two of his designs open to the public: the other is the Kennedy Memorial, Runnymede. *Humphrey Repton* (1752–1818): Ashridge, Haileybury, Wyddial Hall, Lamer, Tewin Water, Panshanger (obliterated because of mineral extraction). *John Tradescant* (d. 1609): Hatfield House*. Accompanied a diplomatic mission to Russia and Algiers to bring back rare plants (including apricot).

Gardens Open certain weekends during summer: Abbots House, Abbots Langley; Great Sarratt Hall; Odsey Park, Ashwell; Thundridge Hill House, Cold Christmas Lane, Ware; Bromley Hall, Standon; Ashridge House; Furneux Pelham Gardens; Moor Place; Much Hadham; Benington Lordship; Shaw's Corner, Ayot St Lawrence;

Little Offley; Great Offley; Knebworth House; St Paul's Waldenbury*.

Gilbey, Sir Walter (1831–1914) Gilbey's Gin. Born 11 Windhill, Bishop's Stortford, sixth of seven children. His father ran passenger coaches to London. 1858: married Ellen Parish, daughter of the landlord, White Horse Inn, North Street. Started business as a wine importer. A regular client was Charles Dickens, whose framed cheques hung in the director's dining room at Gilbey's head office, Harlow. Gilbey became successful because he was the first* to sell wine by the bottle (as opposed to the case) and in 1860 Chancellor of the Exchequer William Gladstone permitted the sale of wine in shops. 1868: bought the title Lord of the Manor of Bishop's Stortford. 1895: gave land in Rye Street to build the town's first hospital, created Hockerill Park and golf course. 1896: death of his wife. He built the almshouses in South Street in her memory and named King's Cottages in recognition of his close association with royalty. Buried alongside his wife in New Cemetery, Apton Road.

Gilston Park Eastwick New Place was built in 1550. All that remains is the porch with a bust of Elizabeth I in a niche, stables and barn. 1701: rebuilt by Colonel Plumer of Blakesware, Widford. 1782: rebuilt by James Wyatt. The lake (part of the River Stort) and planting are by Capability Brown. 1830: Robert Plumer Ward, High Sheriff of Hertfordshire, brought to New Place a priceless collection of paintings, objects d'art and a library of 4,000 books. The famous Blakesware Caesars, written about by Charles Lamb*, stood on pedestals in the Octagon Hall, the floor of which was covered by a carpet woven to shape in Constantinople. 1831: when his three daughters and then his wife died within a short time of one another, Robert soon afterwards leased the house with its contents for £2,000 p.a. 1851: the estate was bought by John Hodgson, who demolished the house and auctioned the contents. The staircase went to Rye House. The present house was designed by Philip Hardwick. Some linenfold oak panelling, a Tudor mantelpiece and other carvings were incorporated into it. 1939: billet for army officers and RAF. 1947: house bought by Charles O'Brien, who ran it as a hotel and country club. 1962: taken over by Smith & Nephew.

Girton College Embryo founded in Hitchin by Emily Davies (1830–1921), who battled for university education for women. Aunt to Arthur Llewellyn Davies, great-aunt to the five brothers of J.M. Barrie*'s *Peter Pan* fame. She petitioned the University of London to accept women, but without success, so in 1867 founded her own University College for Women. She looked at premises in Baldock and Stevenage before renting Benslow House, Hitchin. The place where she really needed to be for women to compete with men was Cambridge, so she raised £7,000 (George Eliot* sent a donation)

Benslow House, Hitchin, Britain's first women's college.

to build a college near Girton. It opened in 1874. Benslow House is now a nursing home.

Gladstone, Herbert (1854–1930) Statesman. Youngest son of W.E. Gladstone, Prime Minister. 1916: retired to the manor house, Dane End, Little Munden, where he lived until his death. He was popular with villagers, who nicknamed him Lordy (of the manor). Thirty years after his death, in 1960 the estate was sold for housing and became the hamlet of Dane End, which has superseded Little Munden on maps.

Glis glis Peculiar to Tring (environs). Latin name for edible dormouse (the Romans kept them in cages and fattened them). They look like a small squirrels with big eyes. Loveable antics include running up windows and sliding down again. One of Britain's rarest introduced mammals. 1902: Walter Rothschild released six in Tring Park. Dubbed Seven Sleepers because they hibernate for seven months, and move inside for the winter, choosing lofts and sheds rather than nests. If you hear bumps in the night, remember that they are protected and must not be killed or released.

Godiva, Lady Story first* recorded (in Latin) in the twelfth century by Roger of Wendover, a monk at St Albans. Matthew Paris* updated the story in the thirteenth century. As the abbey stood at an important road junction, Roger may have heard the story from travellers. Lady Godiva was the wife of Leofric, Earl of Mercia. When he imposed an oppressive tax to pay for Canute's bodyguard and she asked him to rescind it, he reputedly said that before that happened he would see her ride naked through Coventry.

Godwin, William (1756–1836) Political writer. Until he no longer believed in God and the congregation sacked him, minister of the Congregational Independent Chapel, Dead Lane, Ware. Visited Scott's* grotto. 1779: he left to live in poverty, devoting himself to literature. Husband of Mary Wollstonecraft, father of Mary (*Frankenstein*) Shelley, father-in-law of Percy Bysshe Shelley, stepfather of Claire Clairmont, step-grandfather of Allegra Byron, friend of Charles Lamb*. A great influence on Shelley, Wordsworth, Hazlitt and Robert Owen.

Goffs or Gough's Oak Goff's (or more correctly Gough's) descendants, the Goughs still live in Goffs House. Called by Lamb* 'the monster of Cheshunt', the oak was large enough for several people to stand inside its hollow trunk. After the 1,000-year-old tree fell during a gale in 1950, a new one was planted outside Goffs Oak Hotel.

Goldings Goldings, in Waterford, near Hertford, was the name of the country seat of Robert Smith. 1869: Smith wanted the road to be positioned away from his house, so he built a new one. Bramfield and Watton Roads were moved to bring the River Beane into the park; Mole Wood stream was tapped to feed Goldings Canal. A new estate road was also built. 1872: Smith rebuilt Goldings on higher ground away from river mists. Goldings Mark III, a vast red-brick mansion completed in 1877, was the family's home for fifty years. 1922: 260 Barnardo Boys from Stepney, led by their own band, marched from Hertford station to take up residence. The Prince of Wales (later Edward VIII) attended the official opening of the William Baker Technical School and British Pathé News covered the ceremony. 1967: Goldings was sold to the County Council. 1997: sold to Harinbrook Properties, which turned the house into flats and developed the grounds.

Grace, W.G. (1848–1915) Surgeon and genius cricketer. In 1896 Michael Grace, a relative, bought Porters, Hawksmoor*'s old home in Shenley. He asked Grace to lay out a cricket ground the same dimensions as the Oval. This is probably why Cecil Raphael, the next owner, purchased it: his son John captained Sussex. The cricket ground is still there.

Grand Union Canal 1793, Birmingham to London. The canal runs parallel to the railway between King's Langley and Northampton. It runs through Apsley, Hemel, Berkhamsted and Tring. John Dickinson*, Rose's Lime Juice*, and Ovaltine* all traded along its banks, and it was busy until the railways came. Now used for pleasure.

Great Amwell Emma's Well (Domesday Book: Eame Well). Until the 1990s, with nearby Chad Well, this was the main source of London's drinking water via the New River*. Mary Lamb*, one of the earliest children's authors, set *Mrs Leicester's School* here. Izaak Walton* and John Scott* both wrote lovingly about it.

Great Bed of Ware The carved oak four-poster on which guests engraved their initials (it is covered with graffiti and wax seals) measures 11ft square and 7ft high. It has a magnificently carved head, work-of-art canopy and richly decorated bedposts. The number of sleepers it could accommodate depends on who is writing. 1596: Prince Ludwig: 'There was in Wahr a bed so spacious that four couples could lie in it comfortably without touching each other.' Most say it could sleep twelve. Among many stories about it is that there were three, the first built for the very tall Edward IV* (1442–83), the second in 1590, the third in 1650. If true, the one in Shakespeare's *Twelfth Night* was the second: Sir Toby Belch urges Sir Andrew Aguecheek to write to Olivia telling 'as many lies as will lie thy sheet of paper although the sheet were big enough for the bed of Ware'. 1700: owned by the Crown inn, where writer Ned Ward complained of being ripped off. 1764:

Great Amwell, the source of the New River.

owned by the Saracen's Head. The bed was in Ware until 1890 when it was bought by Rye House* Hotel. In 1931 it was bought by the Victoria and Albert Museum, where it is on permanent display. Some sources say it looks Bavarian because it was made by a German craftsman for Owen of Ware Park, others that it was made by a local man, Jonas Fosbrooke and that the drapes cost more than the bed. Of carved oak with inlays of marquetry, it was originally painted and features the swans for which Ware was famous. Ware Museum, which plans to exhibit it in 2008, intended to build a replica but the idea seems to have been dropped.

Great Offley Matthew Paris, historian-monk of St Albans, said that Offa*, King of Mercia, lived here until 'he was called to his rest'. Offley Place may be on the site of Offa's palace. Built in the seventeenth century for Sir Richard Spencer, it was added to in the eighteenth century when Sir Thomas Salusbury, high court judge, owned it. He died in 1773 and his monument is in the church. His niece, Hester Thrale* (née Salusbury) became a patron of Dr Johnson. In the nineteenth century George Hughes (1821–72) and his wife, Anne (née Salusbury) lived here. Their son Herbert inherited Offley. When he died the house passed to his son, Guy, who sold it in 1928. Owned today by the County Council, it is used for conferences and weddings and as a residential training centre. Restaurant is open to the public for lunch.

Greene, Graham (1904–91) Novelist. Born in Berkhamsted; his father was headmaster of Collegiate School. He played Russian roulette on the common with a loaded gun. He worked for MI6 and was a friend of spies Kim Philby and Guy Burgess. His first two novels failed; the third, *The Man Within*, written at home in Berkhamsted,

was a success. Berkhamsted appears in *The Human Factor* and in his autobiography *A Sort of Life*. The Graham Greene Society publishes *A Sort of Newsletter*. Graham Greene Birthplace Trust Festival every September.

Grove, The Watford. Grade II, eighteenth-century house, now a hotel. One of the most fashionable homes in the UK, standing in 300 acres with two lakes, with the Gade and the Grand Union Canal running through the grounds; invitations were sought after. Architect Edward Blore redesigned the ground floor and added a huge staircase and a third floor to display Earl Clarendon's collection of Old Master paintings. George III, the Queen and court stayed here, as did the Duke of Wellington. Because it is conveniently near London, this is where the aristos' 'weekend in the country' started. Queen Victoria, Edward VII, Horace Walpole, Lord Palmerston *et al.* would arrive on Saturday and return to London on Monday morning. This was one of the great political houses of the nineteenth century where the great and the good resolved the issues of the day. Someone who didn't stay was the artist George Stubbs. When Lord Clarendon commissioned him to paint his horses he preferred his own bed, so commuted from Edgware each day on the Watford coach. One day he missed it and walked the 18 miles. Vita Sackville West (1892–1962), writer and gardener, often stayed. In 1912 she spent Christmas here so as to attend the grand New Year Ball at Hatfield House, where she accepted Harold Nicholson's marriage proposal.

Gunpowder Plot King James I was staying at Royston* when the Catholic Lord Monteagle of Furneux Pelham received the famous letter (now in The National Archives) from his brother-in-law Francis

Tresham, warning him not to attend parliament on 5 November 1605. James, grateful to Monteagle for advising him of the danger, gave him an annuity of £500 for life plus lands worth a further £200 p.a. Conspiracy theories spread that the plot had been hatched by Monteagle and that Tresham had been set up.

Gwyn, Nell (1650–87) Mistress of Charles II. Said to have stayed with Charles at the George Inn, Bishop's Stortford, Salisbury Hall, London Colney and also at Sir Henry Guy's new Tring Manor designed for Guy by Sir Christopher Wren. There is an eighteenth-century 50ft-high Nell Gwyn obelisk in the grounds of Tring Manor, but no one knows why. Suggestions include that it commemorates her visits, commemorates her dog, shows the then owner's (William Gore's) status and his pride in the 'royal' connection.

H

Haileybury College Hertford Heath. Designed in 1806 for the East India Company by 27-year-old William Wilkins (1778–1839). The gardens were by Repton. For fifty years it was a training college for civil servants bound for India, but when they were no longer needed, it reopened as a public school. Thomas Malthus, who said famines and calamities are necessary to check population growth, was a tutor here in economics and demographics. The chapel's enormous dome is by Sir Arthur Blomfield, whose nephew, Sir Reginald Blomfield, was a pupil here. Old Boys include Clement Attlee, Alan Ayckbourn, Rudyard Kipling, John McCarthy, Stirling Moss and Rex Whistler.

Handley Page Aircraft factory, founded by Sir Frederick Handley Page (1885–1962). 1930: new factory and airfield established at Radlett*. Made the famous Halifax (nicknamed the Hally or Hallibag), which, with the Lancaster, conducted RAF night bombing raids. It was officially named in September 1941 by Lord Halifax, Foreign Secretary. The last Handley Page design, the Jetstream, flew in 1967, but the company was in receivership by 1970. There is a memorial stone to Sir Handley Page at the former entrance to Radlett* aerodrome.

Hardy, Thomas (1840–1928) Novelist. His uncle Sharpe, born in St Ippollitts*, married his mother's sister, Martha Hands. They lived in Hitchin until uncle Sharpe started work at Hatfield House, where Hardy's mother brought Thomas to stay for a month. He attended a school in Fore Street.

Harpenden Novelist Elizabeth Bowen* lived here, as did the traitor Esterhazy*. Synonymous with Rothamsted. With a common of 238 acres, the town once had its own racecourse. It is famous now for its Highland Gathering in July, the largest outside Scotland (pipe bands, dancing, caber tossing, etc.). Also in July a classic car rally is held on the common. Artificial fertiliser was invented by Sir John Bennet Lawes (1814–1900), gentleman farmer and chemist, who lived on the family estate at Rothamsted. In 1842 he put animal bones treated with acid (super-phosphate of lime) on a field of turnips and got double the yield. Rothamsted Biotechnology and Biological Sciences Research Council now employs 500 scientists.

Harrison, George (1943–2001) Beatle. Purchased Piggot's Manor, Aldenham*, for use as a Krishna Hindu Temple and renamed it Bhaktivedanta.

Hartsbourne Manor Bushey Heath. Home of Maxine Elliott (1868–1940), American actress, who invented the name Maxine. Dubbed 'Queen of Herts'. A close friend of Jenny Churchill* and Alice Keppel, mistress of Edward VII, Maxine was also rumoured to be the King's mistress. She built the King's Suite adjoining her room. Anyone who was anyone came here: many arrived by plane, a cause of much wonder, the whole of Bushey turning out to see them land. She sold Hartsbourne in 1923. It is now a country club.

Hatfield 970: King Edgar gave land to the monks of Ely. 1285: St Etheldreda's built. 1497: the Bishop of Ely built a palace, taken over by Henry VIII in the sixteenth century. Elizabeth I was confined here for three years during her sister's reign, and left here as monarch in 1558. She held her first Council in the Great Hall. The opening of the de Havilland aircraft factory in the 1930s meant rapid growth of the town. As birthplace of the Mosquito, Comet and Trident, it is forever linked with the history of aviation. Post-war, Hatfield became one of eight New Towns* around London. 1960: de Havilland taken over by Hawker Siddeley. 1977: Hawker Siddeley Aviation, British Aircraft Corporation and Scottish Aviation nationalised to become British Aerospace (BAe). They were the district's largest employers until the factory closed in 1993. 1986: Hatfield Tunnel, the longest cut-and-cover road tunnel in Europe, built. The town is unfortunately associated with a rail crash in October 2000, in which four people died when the London-to-Leeds express derailed at a speed of 115mph.

Hatfield Aerodrome De Havilland knew the only way to leapfrog the US in civil aviation after the Second World War was to adopt jet propulsion. The Comet, the world's first jet airliner, was born. 1930: site bought by de Havilland. 1930s: pioneering aircraft built, e.g. Tiger Moth, Rapide and many others (visitors to nearby Duxford can book a flight on both). 1935: training school for RAF pilots. 1939: Amy Johnson* based here. 1941: first Mosquito flight. 1943: double-cross sabotage raid: MI5/SS agent 'Zigzag' Eddie Chapman* made a spoof 'attack'. 1947: new runway built. 1952: Comet flight test hangar built, the largest aluminium building in the world at 200 × 330ft with doors 45ft high (a listed building, now a sports centre for University of Hertfordshire). 1994: airfield closed. 2005: site used for University of Hertfordshire, commercial, leisure and residential development. The control tower is now used as offices.

Hatfield House James I lusted after Theobalds* and persuaded Robert Cecil, 1st Earl

Hatfield House.

of Salisbury, to swap it for the old Bishop's Palace at Hatfield. Cecil built a new palace (the present one) at a cost of £38,000, parts of it designed by Inigo Jones, and employed John Tradescant to lay out the gardens. He was sent to Europe to bring back trees, bulbs and plants never before seen in England. His designs included orchards, fountains, scented walkways, parterres, terraces, herb gardens and a maze (the Herb, Knot and Wilderness Gardens can be seen when the house is open). The result was stunning, but Cecil died before it was finished. Inside the house are Elizabeth I's yellow silk stockings, hat, letters and two world-famous portraits by court painters: one by Nicholas Hilliard with an ermine (the Ermine Portrait), the other showing the Queen in a dress patterned with eyes and ears and with the inscription *non sine souls iris* – no rainbow without the sun (the Rainbow Portrait). The 3rd Marquess of Salisbury was Queen Victoria's favourite PM. He held office three times. Hatfield House is now home to the 7th Marquess and the location for the *Batman* films.

Hawking, Professor Stephen (b. 1942) Lucasian Professor of Mathematics, University of Cambridge. Genius physicist and author of *A Brief History of Time*, world famous for work on black holes and the big bang theory, for triumphing over motor neurone disease, and for making science popular. His family moved to St Albans when he was eight. His father wanted him to go to Westminster School but he was ill on the day of the entrance exam, so he went to St Albans School instead. He loved maths, but his father urged him to study chemistry as he wanted him to go to his old college, University College, Oxford, which had no Fellow in Mathematics.

Hawksmoor, Nicholas (1661–1736) Architect, and pupil of Christopher Wren. He helped design St Paul's Cathedral and Westminster Abbey. 1694: supervised construction of Royal Naval Hospital, Greenwich. 1711: appointed surveyor of fifty new London churches (to be rebuilt after the loss of eighty-seven churches in the Great Fire of London), of which he designed six. 1715: bought Porters mansion in Shenley (the Porter family lived there at least until the fifteenth century). He loved it so much that he asked to be buried in nearby St Botolph's. His monument is in the churchyard. A later owner of Porters was Lord Howe, Admiral of the Fleet. In the 1930s it was surrounded by Shenley Mental Hospital. The hospital has come and gone, but Porters, divided into private apartments, remains.

Professor Stephen Hawking.

Hemel Hempstead Has the famous 'Magic Roundabout'*. 705: Offa gave land here to the Bishop of London. 1066: William I gave it to his half-brother Robert, Count of Mortain. St Mary's, which dates from 1140, has an amazing spire, 130ft high and similar to that of Salisbury Cathedral, built at about the same time. It is said that Henry VIII and Anne Boleyn stayed at The Bury in Gadebridge Park. William Cobbett* liked Hemel, especially the canal. Created a New Town after the war. July 1952: Queen Elizabeth laid the foundation stone of St Barnabas, Adeyfield. 1968: Kodak based its headquarters in Station Road. The prestigious landmark nineteen-storey office block was completed 1971. In front is a cast of Rodin's *Monument to Balzac*.

Henry I (1068–1135) Youngest son of William I, his only son born in England. Killed his brothers to get the Crown, and took Berkhamsted Castle from its builder, his uncle Robert, Count of Mortain. Sometimes held court there. With Queen Matilda and their son William, his heir, also stayed often at St Albans.

Henry II (1133–89). Apologised to St Albans Abbey for the murder of Becket and gave it Brickendon. 1163: spent Christmas at Berkhamsted Castle. 1170: spent Christmas at Hertford Castle (which he modernised).

Henry III (1207–72) 1225: demolished Anstey Castle; spent Easter at St Albans. 1247: stayed a week at St Albans. 1252: stayed with son Edward at St Albans. 1257: stayed at St Albans with Edward, also with Queen Eleanor in March, October and November. 1264: Queen Eleanor stayed in St Albans.

Henry IV (1367–1413) Henry Bolingbroke (born at Bolingbroke Castle, Lincolnshire). Usurper, had Richard II murdered. 1401: gave Langley Palace to his wife Joan (daughter of Charles of Navarre), who stayed there often. 1403: at Hertford Castle with his family.

Henry V (1387–1422) 1413: Easter at King's Langley. 1415: Sir William Hungerford recruited soldiers from Hitchin to fight for Henry at Agincourt.

Henry VI (1421–71) Only child of Henry V and Catherine de Valois, half-brother of Edmund and Jasper Tudor. Visited the county frequently. 1437: at Hertford Castle. 1445: married Margaret of Anjou and gave her Hertford Castle as a wedding present. They stayed there often. 1450: spent Easter at St Albans. Gave his gown to the abbey to raise funds, then bought it back. 22 May 1455: First Battle* of St Albans, Henry v. Richard, Duke of York; York wins. 1461: Second Battle of St Albans; Henry v. Edward, Duke of York (Edward's father Richard now dead); Henry wins. 1471: Battle of Barnet; Edward v. Warwick. Edward wins and proclaimed king. Henry is executed.

Henry VIII (1491–1547) 1515: modernised Hertford Castle. 1523: stayed at Angel Vaults, Hitchin (now demolished). 1525: built Hunsdon House; said to have visited Cardinal Wolsey at Great Wymondley. 1528: stayed at Hertford Castle, Hatfield House, Hunsdon and Tyttenhanger. 1530: spent Christmas at Ashridge. 1532: rebuilt Hunsdon.

Heritage Open Days September. *Berkhamsted*: Town Hall. *Harpenden*: Rothamsted Manor, St Nicholas' Church. *Hatfield*: Mill Green Museum, St Etheldreda's. *Hemel Hempstead*: St Mary's. *Hertford*: County Hall, Castle. *Hitchin*: British Schools Museum, Holy Saviour, St Mary's, The Biggin, Princess Helena College, Tilehouse Street Baptist Church. *St Albans*: Abbey Gateway, Clock Tower, Comfort Hotel, Kyngston House, Redbournbury Watermill, Sopwell Nunnery,

Cathedral, Organ Museum, Town Hall, Old Town Hall. *Tring*: Tring Park. *Ware*: Fanhams Hall, Place House, Scott's Grotto, Priory. *Welwyn*: St Peter's, Roman Baths.

Hertford County town. Four rivers meet here: the Mimram, Rib, Beane and Lea. Fortress during the 200 years that the Anglo-Saxons fought the Danes, who sailed from London up the Lea and reached Ware. 673: Archbishop of Canterbury held the first* Synod* of the English Church here. Five bishops representing East Anglia, Kent, Mercia, Northumbria and Wessex agreed on diocesan boundaries and established the Church in England. There is a memorial stone in front of Hertford Castle. 1669: the first* purpose-built Friends'* Meeting House (Quakers) founded by George Fox* is still here. Wesley* preached here often.

Hertford Castle Norman motte, walls and gate. 1170: Henry II built the present castle with a 7ft-thick wall. 1216: played a key role in the Barons' struggles against King John, when he took the castle and the Barons asked the French for help. When John died the castle was ceded to the French Dauphin. 1346: King David of Scotland, taken prisoner at Nevills Cross with his wife Queen Joan (sister of Edward III), was imprisoned here. 1359: Edward III gave the castle to his first son, Edward the Black Prince, who won the battles of Crécy and Poitiers and captured King John of France and brought him to the castle. When the Black Prince died Edward gave the castle to another son, John of Gaunt (Ghent). As the guardian of his brother's son, Richard II – the boy king – he lived here as the most powerful, most hated man in England and effectively ruled the country. He married the daughter of the Duke of Lancaster, the wealthiest duke in England and incorporated the castle into the Duchy. He married the

second of his three wives, Constanza of Castile, a Spanish princess, here. His third wife, the love of his life, was Katherine Swynford. Some of her servants were buried in St Nicholas (Maidenhead Street). 1420: Henry V gave the castle to his wife, Catherine de Valois. Many of their fourteen months of married life were spent here. 1455: Henry VI gave it to his wife, Margaret of Anjou. She was put under house arrest here by the Duke of York. As Edward IV, he gave it to his wife, Elizabeth Woodville, and built the gatehouse. 1528: Henry VIII made improvements and stayed here with Catherine of Aragon and her lady-in-waiting Anne Boleyn. Edward VI spent much of his childhood here, as did Elizabeth I. Her book of prayers in the British Museum is inscribed 'Hertford 1535'. Her Privy Council, law courts and parliament relocated here for ten years (1582–92) when London was ravaged by plague (hence Parliament Square). Queens Road is so named because she often enjoyed the view from the hilltop spot now known as Queen's Bench. Royal association ended after Elizabeth's death. In 1603 James I gave the castle to his son Charles, who gave it to William Cecil, 2nd Earl of Salisbury, whose descendants still own it. 1911: Lord Salisbury leased it to the Town Council, the Gatehouse was converted into offices and the gardens were opened to the public.

Hertfordshire Building Preservation Trust Formed 1963. By that time chunks of the county's heritage had already disappeared (the Victoria and Albert Museum ran a valedictory exhibition 'The Destruction of the English Country House'). Today the county has 8,000 listed buildings and 175 conservation areas. Triumphs for the Trust include: Cromer Windmill, Ardeley; Place House, Ware; Forge Museum and Victorian Cottage Garden, Much Hadham;

John Walton, blacksmith at Much Hadham Forge.

The Standon Puddingstone.

Amwellbury Dovecote; Dewhurst St Mary School, Cheshunt; The Mustard Pot, Broxbourne; St Mary's Old Church, Thundridge; Broadwater Farm, Stevenage; Bourne Cottage, Widford; Torilla, Wilkins Green Lane, Nast Hyde, Hatfield.

Hertfordshire County Show Redbourn*, every summer. Prize-winning cattle, goats and sheep, international show jumping, sheep shearing, dog shows, falconry, fly fishing, ferret racing, steam engines, vintage agricultural machinery, craft demonstrations, trade stands, flower marquee and local produce food hall.

Hertfordshire Puddingstone (resembles plum pudding). One of the world's rarest stones is peculiar to this county. A glacial conglomerate (natural concrete) formed sixty million years ago, consisting of pebbles cemented by silica. There is a good sample at Standon*. In a county where stone is scarce it was used for church foundations. Lumps of it once marked out the Icknield Way*. Pieces were once carried as lucky charms. Also called the Breeding Stone, locals insisting that if one stone were removed it would grow back and that the more farmers removed it from the fields, the more there was next morning. It is now used for doorstops.

Hertfordshire Spike The county's affectionate term for the lead-covered spire on many churches. So much part of the landscape, many are not aware of it. Because there are

Hertfordshire Spike at Ware.

few local sources of building materials, architects couldn't add the usual stone tower. There is no mention of them in the RIBA archives or in reference books.

Hexton Said to be the first* planned model village. In the nineteenth century John Hodgson, a wealthy shipbroker, bought the manor, razed the village and built a new one to his own design with farms, school, dairy and cottages. Today his dream village has barely changed. He replaced New Place, an Elizabethan house, with Gilston Park (now a research centre for pharmaceuticals). Pevsner: 'The present house, replacing one demolished 1851, is a large asymmetrical mansion of random rubble in the Early Tudor style with Gothic details.' The twelfth-century church, still with its original font, was rebuilt in the sixteenth century and restored by Hodgson. Today, houses are being built in Gilston Park.

Hine, Reginald (1883–1949) Hitchin solicitor, local historian. Born to wealthy parents at Newnham Hall near Baldock. Memorial tapestry in the church made in 1949 by an Ashwell man. There is a memorial garden in Lower Tilehouse Street, Hitchin and a memorial tablet among the ruins of Minsden Chapel (footpath behind Royal Oak on the B656 between Hitchin and Codicote). The county is in his debt for his determination not to let George Chapman* slide into obscurity and for writing the definitive book on Charles Lamb's* connections with the county. Tall, handsome and extrovert, dressing in velvet jackets, flamboyant bow ties, green suits, pink shirts and spats, he had a finger in every pie. He cycled in the rain with an open umbrella. A depressive, he fought off mental instability until the day he jumped in front of a train at Hitchin station. He had hoped to die at Minsden, his favourite place, because, he said, his mind too was in ruins.

Hitchin Once known as Hiche (the Hicce tribe settled on the banks of the Hiz). Situated on a major trade route known to prehistoric travellers. The Romans also knew this area (remains of buildings, utensils and coins). Modern Hitchin began in Saxon times when King Offa* founded a religious house here on the site of St Mary's Church in 792 (second only in size to St Albans Abbey). Simon Jenkins, writing in *The Times*, called it 'the largest and jolliest church in Hertfordshire'. Hitchin was owned by King Harold until taken by William I. It is listed in the Domesday Book as Hiz (hence the river). From then on Hitchin was a royal manor, granted to subjects who excelled in service, e.g. the Baliols. Cromwell billeted 3,000 soldiers here. In 1688 sister princesses Mary and Anne (later queens), daughters

St Mary's Church, Hitchin.

of James II, left court when plots against their father began and are said to have stayed with William Blomfield in Bancroft. Pevsner described Hitchin as being, after St Albans, the most visually satisfying town in the county. Regrettably, the following buildings have been demolished: Angel Vaults, Sun Street (1450 with medieval and sixteenth-century timbering); 114 Bancroft (fifteenth-century Town Hall with panelled canopy unique in town halls); Three Horseshoes, High Street (Tudor); 21 Bridge Street (fifteenth century); Grange, Portmill Lane (part of a Georgian group); Skynner's Almshouses in Bancroft, built in 1670, have survived but, unloved, are barely noticed behind an ugly brick wall. Queen Street slums were cleared in the 1920s and 1930s, which, considering the resulting bleak depressing open space, is a pity. Grandly called St Mary's Square, it is in reality a huge, ugly concrete car park. Behind 64/66 Queen

Street were Hitchin Swimming Baths, filled from the River Hiz.

Hobson's Choice Tom Hobson (1544–1631). Born in Buntingford, he left money to the town in his will. Married to a girl from Ware. He ran livery stables in London and Cambridge, treating his forty horses well and sticking rigidly to a system of strict rotation: when renting out he gave customers the horse nearest the door, 'take it or leave it'. He provided a rental package: horse, saddle, clothes, boots, whips, the lot. John Milton, a Cambridge student, mentioned Hobson in two epitaphs. He was also written about in the *Spectator*.

Hoddesdon Lowewood Museum has a lock of Edward IV's hair. John McAdam* lived here. Earl (Arthur) Balfour (1848–1930), PM and MP for Hertford, went to the Grange Preparatory School (now demolished) before attending Eton. Mrs Faithfull opened the school in 1854 after her husband's death. Arthur, one of five brothers who all attended, was famous for the Balfour Declaration of 1917 which promised Jews a national home in Palestine. He replaced his uncle, the Marquess of Salisbury, as PM. Olympics hero Harold Abrahams (*Chariots of Fire*) also lived here. The Hertfordshire International Film Festival is held annually in Broxbourne Town Hall (which, confusingly, is in Hoddesdon, not Broxbourne).

Holbrook, David (b. 1924) Poet. *Nothing Larger than Life* is his fictionalised autobiography about the twenty years (1954–74) he spent in Ashwell*, where he wrote many poems. One describes the scene from his window, another being in bed when the Queen Mother unexpectedly visited the village in 1969. His anthologies were once on teacher-training college curriculums. 1954: with wife Margot and their two children he rented Phyllis Fordham's house 'Ducklake', available to artistic types willing to be useful in village affairs. He became a parish councillor, obtained a grant for the village hall, started a youth club and gave the village two more children. 1960s: with musician Elizabeth Poston from Rooks Nest, a friend of E.M. Forster*, he wrote a cantata inspired by the graffiti in Ashwell church for the Ashwell Festival. He also wrote the libretto for an opera for young people with music by John Joubert. 1973: moved to Cambridge. Emeritus Fellow of Downing College, Cambridge.

Holmes, Sherlock Fictional detective created by Arthur Conan Doyle in 1887 and killed off by him in 1902. His physical appearance originated in Chipperfield*, where Sidney and Walter Paget, brother illustrators, lived in Brazier House. Sidney, who illustrated Conan Doyle's books, gave the world an enduring image of Holmes

Sherlock Holmes.

when he used Walter as the model. Like Holmes, Walter was tall and thin with small, sharp, piercing eyes and a hawk nose. The famous deerstalker hat was Sidney's own. Walter illustrated books by Rider Haggard and Robert Louis Stevenson.

Hope, Bob (1903–2003) Film star. He claimed to have inherited his sense of humour from his grandfather James, of Hitchin*, a stonemason who worked on the Statue of Liberty in Paris (before it was shipped to New York) and the Royal Courts of Justice in the Strand. William, Bob's father, was also a stonemason and in 1907 followed brothers Frank and Fred to America. Hope said 'I left England at the age of four when I found out I couldn't be king.' 1939: Bob received a letter from Aunt Lucy of Brampton Park Road, who had James living with her, inviting him over. He worked the invitation into his act before boarding the SS *Normandie* for his first trip 'back home'. Years later he wrote in his autobiography: 'We had a great ball in the pub down in Hitchin. I invited all the relatives . . . never seen them before . . . grandfather James got up – he was 96 . . .

introduced everybody, told a couple of jokes and did a little dance so you can see where my ham comes from.' As the *Queen Mary* drew away from Southampton two days before war was declared, James shouted 'See you on my 100th.' 1943: visiting American air bases in Hertfordshire on a morale-boosting tour, he heard his grandfather was ill so went to Hitchin and said 'Come on grandpa, I'm going to take you on stage with me.' James smiled. He died two days later. Hope attended the funeral. 1950s: hosted a party for relatives at the Sun Hotel, Hitchin, and played at Letchworth Golf Club. 1982: golf tournament at Moor Park*. Hosted party for his relatives in Blakemore Hotel, Little Wymondley. 1998: received an honorary knighthood.

Hospitallers Knights of St John. The only pre-Reformation (military) Order to survive in the UK. No longer a Holy Order (Catholic) but Venerable (Church of England St John Ambulance). The head of the Order was a Commander (hence Commandery, e.g. Standon). There was also a Commandery at Broxbourne*. 1309: the Templars were disbanded and their lands were given to the Hospitallers. 1544: Henry VIII confiscated Hospitaller properties during the Reformation.

Howard, Sir Ebenezer (1850–1928). Social reformer, Quaker idealist. Today, his ideas are common sense, in his day they were derided. As a London clerk, appalled by the living and working conditions of the poor, he didn't see why they should not live in nice houses with nice gardens, and if they had to work in factories these too should be nice. He formed the Garden City Association to promote a new kind of town with a clean, pleasant, healthy environment. There were to be clearly defined areas for commerce, industry, housing and agriculture, surrounded by a 'green belt'. His vision became a worldwide blueprint. Alcohol, he said, was detrimental so his ideal town did not sell it. In an age when drunks lay in gutters, many people were attracted to Letchworth because it was dry. Factories were built in locations where smells could be carried away by prevailing winds. He chose Letchworth for his first Garden City (1903) because Weston Hills supplied an abundance of water. He held a competition for the best-designed houses costing £100 at most to be built along Exhibition Road (Nevells Road). The second Garden City was built in Welwyn in 1919.

Hunsdon Before the Reformation the church was dedicated to the Blessed Virgin Mary Our Lady of Hunsdon. Afterwards, as St Dunstan, it was attended by the children of Henry VIII, who lived in Hunsdon House*. The Pump House dates from 1637, the Old House, Widford Road, from 1690 and the village hall is eighteenth century.

Hunsdon Airfield Opened 1941 with 85 Squadron under Wing Commander Peter Townsend*. 1942: first Mosquitos. 1943: John 'Cat's Eyes' Cunningham* commanded the most famous night-fighter formation of the Second World War. July and August 1944: dedicated to interception of V-1 flying bombs. Closed in 1947.

Hunsdon House Between Ware and Sawbridgeworth. Started as a monastery. 1447: Sir William Oldhall built a house (barrel-vaulted cellar still there). 1471: Edward IV* gave it to Thomas Howard, Duke of Norfolk. 1525: Henry VIII* carried out a ten-year building project to create a magnificent palace with a moat (filled in in 1800) for 'the breeding and education of his children in respect of the air'. He stayed often and ate in private in Oldhall's tower. Edward VI's 1546 portrait was painted with the house in the background. Mary Tudor left from here to claim the throne of England. 1559: Elizabeth gave the house to her half-brother Henry Carey and created him Baron Hunsdon. 1623: the French Ambassador allowed Catholics to worship here. When 300 met in an upstairs room, the floor collapsed, hurling them to the floor beneath, which also collapsed, killing 100. Protestants rejoiced, saying it was an act of God; Catholics accused them of sawing through the timbers beforehand. During the Civil War Cromwell took the house. In the nineteenth century a new house was built incorporating the remains of Henry VIII's palace. The present house is one-quarter the size (one wing).

Hunsdon, Lord (1526–96) Henry Carey, 1st Baron Hunsdon. Knight of the Garter, personal bodyguard of Elizabeth I, Privy Counsellor, Lord Chamberlain. She called him 'dear coz', but he was her half-brother, son of Henry VIII and his mistress Mary Boleyn, who went through an arranged marriage with William Carey. It is probable that his sister Catherine, named after the Queen, was also fathered by Henry VIII. When William Carey died, Henry came under the guardianship of his mother's sister, Anne Boleyn. 1559: created Baron by Elizabeth I and given the manors of Hunsdon and Eastwick, with a pension of £4,000 p.a. Buried in Westminster Abbey.

Hunting AD 43: Romans hunted hare and deer. 1066: Normans brought hounds from Gascony (hunting was a royal preserve). 1340: foxes were hunted. Edward I is said to have had the first royal foxhound pack. 1660: after the Restoration hunting grew as a sport and the first trained packs emerged. Game was still the primary quarry. 1793: Mary Amelia, Marchioness of Salisbury (1749–1835), the first woman Master of Foxhounds, hunted with her own pack, the Hertfordshire Hunt, until 1819 (her 70th year). Gilray drew a cartoon of her coming home after the hunt ragged and weary. She died in a fire at Hatfield House. 1831: game laws which restricted hunting were repealed and fox hunting grew in popularity as the new railways allowed hunters such as John Leech* to travel with their horses. 1866: the Hertfordshire Hounds, based at Kinsbourne Green near Harpenden (until 1914), were said to be the finest kennels in Europe. The famous Enfield Chace Hunt met not in Enfield but at Wormley West End. Puckeridge Hunt Master was John Calvert, MP for Hertford until 1808. He was succeeded by his son John of Albury Hall, MP for St Albans. Edward Barclay took over in 1896, followed by son, grandson and great-granddaughter Diana (Pyp). 2005: hunting with dogs was banned.

Huxley, Aldous (1894–1963) Writer. Nephew of Mary Ward* of Stocks*. Named after Aldous Raeburn, a character in *Marcella*, published the year he was born. 1908: at Eton aged 12 when his mother died. From then on his home was with aunt 'Marooe' and his three cousins. In *Eyeless in Gaza* she is Mrs Foxe. Mary hosted holidays for crippled children from London's East End, also mentioned in *Eyeless in Gaza*, where he recalls them hopping around on crutches, with which they threatened the young Wards and Huxleys.

I

Icknield Way 103 miles long. Some parts are prehistoric. It is probably the oldest road in Europe. The Hertfordshire stretch passes through Streatley, Pirton, Ickleford, Wilbury Hill, where there are remains of an ancient fortification, Letchworth, Norton, Baldock, Ashwell, Therfield, Slip End and Royston.

Iron Age (700 BC–AD 43) The county of Hertfordshire is one of the best places in Europe to study the Iron Age. Ravensburgh Castle (400 BC), the largest hill fort in eastern England (22 acres), straddles the Barton Hills near Hexton. It has two entrances and is surrounded by a ditch. Wealthy Iron Age burials include three in Welwyn, two in Baldock and a 'royal' burial in St Albans, one of the most impressive known in Celtic Europe. 2004: an 800 BC Iron Age village was found at Fairfield Park near Hitchin.

J

James I (1566–1625) 1603 Lord Hunsdon* rode to Scotland to tell James he was King of England. On his way to London James stayed at Royston with Robert Chester, whose house he bought to build a royal residence. Cost £4,000. He spent so much time there his ministers found government difficult. It was at Royston that he heard of the Gunpowder Plot* and where he signed Walter Raleigh's death warrant. If it were not for him, the county might still be blessed with great bustards, which he used to hunt on Therfield* Heath. Sir Henry Cock entertained him at Broxbourne Manor. 1605: at Robert Cecil's Theobalds with brother-in-law the King of Denmark. 1607: exchanged the derelict Old Palace, Hatfield, for Theobalds. 1611: established a menagerie at Theobalds. The King of Spain gave him an elephant, camels, rare white baby hinds with their own (human) wet nurse, flying squirrels, sables and falcons. 1625: died at his beloved Theobalds, of which, thanks to Cromwell, nothing is left.

Jennings, Sarah (1660–1744) Duchess of Marlborough. Born at Water End House, Sandridge, near Wheathampstead. 1678: married John Churchill, who loved her passionately until he died. 1688: confidante of Princess Anne, whom she persuaded to depose her father, the Catholic James II. 1683: letters between the Princess and Sarah as 'Mrs Morley' and 'Mrs Freeman' (gossip had it they were lovers). On Anne's accession, appointed Mistress of the Robes and Keeper of the Privy Purse. Sarah introduced a poor relation, Mrs Abigail Marsham (née Hill), to the Queen. Abigail soon had more influence over her than Sarah. Anne was frightened of Sarah, who used to swear at her. The last interview between this strange pair was in April 1710, when Sarah and John Churchill were dismissed. One of Sarah's many properties in St Albans was at Holywell, where the Duke of Marlborough pub now stands.

John, King (1167–1216) Destroyed Bishop's Stortford (Waytemore) and Benington castles. 1213: beginning of democracy in England (for the wealthy) when a council met at St Albans to debate John's misrule. The Shire Reeve (Sheriff) and four men from each town were invited, making it the first* national representative body. The council drafted Magna Carta (Great Charter), which John was forced to sign at Runnymede in 1215 (at the same time he strengthened the castle fortifications at Berkhamsted). When he refused to implement the changes, Hertfordshire became a battleground for the ensuing civil war. The King's men held Hertford, Berkhamsted and Bishop's Stortford while he ravaged the estates of the barons who opposed him. They sought help from the Dauphin of France. 1216: John died and was succeeded by his son, Henry III.

Johns, W.E. (1893–1968). Creator of Biggles. Born in Fairfield Cottage, Molewood Road, Bengeo*. The family picnicked often in The Baulk, Bengeo. He attended Hertford Grammar School (fee-paying), where he was useless at everything except drawing, the piano and rifle practice (army cadets). When he left school in 1908 he wanted to be a soldier, but his father apprenticed him to Hertford Municipal Surveying Department to be a water engineer. When war broke out six years later he was a soldier until he transferred to the RFC and was taken prisoner of war. 1932: appointed editor of *Aviation* magazine, in which James Bigglesworth made his first appearance and became a schoolboys' hero (ninety-six Biggles books). 1963: when the chief librarian at St Pancras banned his books as racist, Johns fell out of fashion. 1993: centenary. A blue plaque on his old home, 41 Cowbridge, was unveiled by his niece, daughter of his brother Russell.

Johnson, Amy (1903–41) Pioneer aviator. 1930: flew solo to Australia in the open cockpit of a de Havilland* Gipsy Moth 'Jason' (now in the Science Museum). 1933: flew in the A$15,000 prize Air Race from England to Melbourne to celebrate the centenary of the state of Victoria. The only planes with the performance necessary to win were American. The DH88 Comet was born of de Havilland's patriotic determination to build a winner. Amy and her husband Jim Mollison called their plane *Black Magic*. The race was won by *Grosvenor House*. 1939: tried to join the RAF as a pilot but was refused and joined the Air Transport Auxiliary as Flight Officer Johnson. Based at Hatfield*, she ferried planes from factories to RAF bases all over the UK. 4 January 1941: died after baling out of an Airspeed Oxford on a flight from Prestwick to Oxford via Blackpool. 14 January 1941: memorial service held at St Martin's-in-the-Fields, London.

Johnson, Dr Samuel (1709–84) Lexicographer. Friend of John Scott* and Edward Young*. 1767: paid for his West Indian servant Francis Barber to be educated at Bishop's Stortford Grammar School for five years and visited him there. Barber's education (wasted) cost Johnson £300. 1774: Johnson, with friend and patron Hester Thrale*, stayed in St Albans.

K

King's Langley One of the most romantic places, historically speaking, in the county. Henry III* built the first palace, Langley on the Gade (hence King's Langley). Edward I rebuilt the palace and founded a Dominican Friary (which survived until Henry VIII's dissolution of the monasteries). 1309: Edward II and his lover Piers Gaveston, spent Christmas together at Langley. 1341: Edward III's fifth son, Edmund, was born here while work on the palace, supervised by his mother Philippa (of Hainault), was in full swing. 1349: during the Black Death the seat of government was moved here from London. It was in the Rose Garden here that Shakespeare set the scene in *Richard II* in which the Queen hears of the usurper Bolingbroke's success. 1431: palace rebuilt. 1487: Cecily, Duchess of York, living at Berkhamsted Castle, granted the lordship of King's Langley to Ralph Verners of Aldbury. 1538: last used by royalty. 1970s: excavation in the grounds of the Rudolf Steiner School revealed an impressive wine cellar (1276), built when Edward I lived here. Almost nothing now remains of a palace complex that was as grand as Westminster Abbey. Inside All Saints' is the tomb of Edmund of Langley.

Knebworth House Known the world over for rock concerts. First, in 1974, were the Doobie Brothers and Van Morrison. The Rolling Stones were followed by Queen, Led Zeppelin, Pink Floyd, the Beach Boys, Oasis and, in 2004, Robbie Williams. Seat of the Lyttons since 1490, when Sir Robert Lytton* bought the estate. Dickens* performed here with his amateur theatrical group. In one bedroom is a cupboard, the original of Jip's kennel in *David Copperfield*. In 1990 a shoe dated 1710, placed in the wall for luck, was replaced with a trainer and CD of a pop concert held at Knebworth. 'That should puzzle some future generation!' said Lord Cobbold. The dining room and library were redesigned in 1908 by family member Edwin Lutyens*. Described as Gothic Revivalist, a Disneyland Magic Kingdom, because of its towers, turrets, cupolas and crenellations, the exterior was started in 1810 by Elizabeth Bulwer-Lytton and completed by her son, the novelist Edward Bulwer-Lytton. The banqueting hall is Tudor. Bulwer-Lytton's study remains as he knew it, complete with the crystal ball he gazed into and the love poem he wrote at age 15 to Lady Caroline Lamb*. On International Women's Day, Stevenage Labour MP Barbara Follett lays flowers on the mausoleum tomb of suffragette Constance Lytton in Knebworth Park. Lady Constance, born in 1869, daughter of Robert, 1st Earl Lytton, was often arrested during demonstrations. Furious at receiving special treatment because of her rank, she changed her name. Her health was damaged by hunger strikes in jail. After a stroke in 1911 she concentrated on writing on women's rights and lived with her mother in Park Lane, Knebworth, where she died in 1923. Lord (David) and Lady (Chrissie) Cobbold wrote *Board Meetings in the Bath* about the highs and lows of inheriting, running and saving Knebworth.

Knox-Johnston, Sir Robin (b. 1939) World-famous yachtsman. Often visits his birthplace, Berkhamsted, where he attended the Collegiate School. 2004: he attended the opening of the state-of-the-art Sports Centre named in his honour and donated the Golden Globe, awarded to him as the first person to sail single-handed non-stop around the world (Sir Francis Chichester, in *Gypsy Moth IV*, 1967, stopped for a refit).

Kubrick, Stanley (1929–99) Genius film director. In 1960 he came from America to film *Lolita* and never went back. In 1979 he bought Childwickbury, a 172-acre estate near St Albans. His daughters Katharina, Anya and Vivian were educated locally. He put a stop to the showing of *A Clockwork Orange* in the UK after he and his family received serious threats. He died a week after his last film, *Eyes Wide Shut*, was delivered to Warner Brothers. Stars of the film Tom Cruise and then his wife Nicole Kidman attended his funeral with Steven Spielberg and many other Hollywood friends. He is buried in his beloved garden at

Stanley Kubrick.

Childwickbury. Every summer his widow, Christiane, an artist of standing, holds the Childwickbury Arts Fair in the grounds.

L

Lamb, Lady Caroline (1785–1828) One of the Spencers of Althorp. It is unlikely anyone would have heard of her had she not married William Lamb of Brocket* Park (Lord Melbourne) or had a love affair with Byron. She wrote *Glenarvon* castigating him and left us the memorable description 'mad, bad and dangerous to know'. She, mother-in-law Lady Melbourne and sister-in-law Lady Emily Cowper (later Lady Palmerston) between them bedded most of Regency London.

Lamb, Charles (1775–1834) Writer, inventor of the personal essay. Many Hertfordshire connections. His mother and grandparents came from Hitchin*, where Mary Bruton married Edward Field in St Mary's in 1736. His mother, Elizabeth Field, was baptised there. When Edward died, Mary became housekeeper at Blakesware (now demolished), Widford*. Charles and his sister Mary often stayed with her and recalled happy times in their writing. At nearby Blenheim Cottage lived Ann Simmons, whom Charles courted for seven years but never married. From his uncle and godfather, Francis Field, he inherited Button Snap, Westmill*.

Lamer (possibly Lee Mere – the river is nearby) Near Wheathampstead. Gardens by Repton. 1618: John Garrard gave this and Ayot Place to his son John, of Waterend. 1761: new house built by Sir Bennett Garrard. 1936: new house built. Apsley Cherry* Garrard lived here most of his life. 1949: house partly demolished. 1953: estate sold. Part of the old walled garden and gateway are said to survive, along with the coachhouse/stables and ice-house. A 1717 bell inscribed 'Sir Samuel Garrard – his bell' is said to be still in the rear courtyard.

Lea, River Very important in the history of England. It formed the boundary finally settled between the Anglo-Saxons and the invading Danes. All land to the north was Danelaw, that to the south formed the kingdom of Wessex. Source at Luton; tributaries the Mimram, Beane, Rib and Stort. Passes through Harpenden, Wheat-hampstead, St Albans, Water End, Lemsford and into Brocket Hall (Lord Melbourne wanted an impressive water feature) between Hatfield and Welwyn Garden City. At Hertford the river splits. The wider, faster water running past Folly Island on the south side is the Lea Navigation. The original Lea runs on the northern side and reconnects with the Navigation at Hertford basin.

Charles Lamb plaque outside Button Snap, Westmill.

Leavesden Airfield 1940: King George V school playing fields requisitioned. Mosquitos and Halifax bombers assembled here. 1946: de Havilland Engine Co. 1960: Bristol Siddeley Engines. 1966: Rolls-Royce Small Engine Division. 1994: factory closed.

Leavesden Film Studios Built on the site of the Rolls-Royce factory in 1995. The UK's first media park, with first purpose-built studios in fifty years, cost £400 million. Part of the county's film and media industry infra-structure for hundreds of film-, television- and media-related companies. *Titanic, The Beach, Sleepy Hollow, Star Wars, Golden Eye, Harry Potter* were all filmed here. Large public park with conservation areas and amphitheatre with community and education resources.

Le Carré, John (b. 1931) Novelist David Cornwell. He and Dick Clements of Clements of Watford department store were fellow ski racers representing Britain in Switzerland in 1951 and are still friends. When Clements settled in Sarratt*, Le Carré decided to set his spy school there and used a gravestone in the churchyard for dead letter drops. Cornwell writes about their friendship in *Sarratt and the Draper of Watford*. In the 1960s Cornwell's boss accused him of being a square, so when he started to write he called himself Le Carré – French for square.

Leech, John (1817–64) *Punch* cartoonist. Loved the county and hunting*. 1852: letter to a friend: 'Look in this week's *Punch* for a sketch of Royston Hills.' 1858: when the railway from King's Cross to Baldock opened he hopped on a train with his horse and stayed at the White Horse Inn. He needed to be near Hitchin (had no station then) to ride to hounds with the Puckeridge Hunt. Also stayed with friends in Barley*.

Letchworth Garden City The world's first* Garden City was started in 1903 to test Ebenezer Howard's* ideas. All profits were ploughed back into the town. A century later, owned by Letchworth Garden City Heritage Foundation with charity status, the principle still stands. A unique example of planned development, it spawned imitations the world over and attracts visitors from around the world to study it. It once attracted bohemians and was the butt of cartoons in national newspapers. Esperanto-speaking cranks with long hair and beards wore togas, smocks and sandals. Letchworth was avant-garde, with vegetarians, animal rights activists (they tried to free the lions from a visiting circus) and cult religions. A Fabian was appointed head of its first school and a woman made news by refusing to pay her rates until she was given the vote. Annie Besant, trade union activist, laid the foundation stone for St Christopher's, one of the most progressive schools in Britain. Annie Lawrence's Cloisters was a residential summer school where guests wore monks' habits, wrote poetry, slept in hammocks, swam in the pool to greet the dawn and ate al fresco. During the First World War the *Daily Mail* claimed Letchworth was a haven for communists when 200 locals were jailed as conscientious objectors. Today a Conservative MP holds the seat.

Lister, Joseph (1827–1912) Quaker doctor who invented antiseptic surgery. His father invented the microscope. He was the first to sterilise surgical instruments and to use carbolic acid to sterilise cuts and wounds. In his lifetime the death rate during and following surgery dropped from 80 per cent to almost nil. Aged 5, Joseph was sent to board at Isaac Brown Quaker Academy in Hitchin. The school closed in 1845. The Lord Lister pub is on the site.

Little Berkhamsted Known for the Folly*, Stratton's Observatory, Bishop Ken* and St Andrew's stained-glass windows by William Morris. In 1571 the Rector was Mr Hughes. His daughter Jane married Thomas Ken, a lawyer. Their daughter Ann married Izaac Walton*. When Jane died, Thomas married again and son Thomas was born here. Thomas Ken* Jnr became a bishop and is commemorated inside the church. During the Second World War Bertram Mills of circus fame bought the manor house. Pop singers Adam Ant and Donovan both lived here.

Little Hadham Arthur, Lord Capel (1610–49), MP for Herts, Royalist leader, raised a troop for Charles I against Cromwell. He was put in the Tower and beheaded. His heart was placed in a box and at the Restoration presented to Charles II. His son Arthur Capel, Earl of Essex, at first fought for Charles II but, disenchanted with Catholic peers at court, also ended up in the Tower. Water at Church End is purified, filtered through 500ft of chalky bedrock, bottled and sold in supermarkets as Hadham Water.

Little Ken Charles II's nickname for his Royal Chaplain. Bishop Thomas Ken (1637–1711) was born at Little Berkhamsted*. His half-sister married Izaac Walton*. Ken, who wrote the famous hymn *Awake My Soul and With the Sun*, was a close friend of Pepys*. Chaplain to Princess Mary, daughter of James II. He was one of the Magnificent Seven bishops who refused to read James II's 1688 Declaration of Indulgence from the pulpit. Although opposed to the Catholic James, he refused to swear allegiance to William and Mary and so was ousted from office.

Little Miss Muffet Dr Moffet/Moufet (1553–1604) of Muffet's Farm (Moffatts is on the site), Brookmans Park. One of Elizabeth I's favourites and personal physician of the Earl of Essex. A keen amateur entomologist and poet, it is thought he wrote 'Little Miss Muffet' in the 1580s when his daughter Patience was frightened by a spider. He suggested that asthmatics should inhale sulphur fumes – it worked.

Lord Lieutenant of Hertfordshire Her Majesty's representative in the county, responsible for receiving members of the Royal Family during visits and overseeing arrangements concerning their programmes.

Lucas, James (1813–74) Lived at Elmwood House, Redcoats Farm, Little Wymondley (demolished). Most famous eccentric in Victorian Britain. When his mother died he refused to let the undertakers in (they broke down the door). He locked himself in for 25 years. When Dickens was staying with Bulwer-Lytton, he went to look at him. Lucas, who loathed Dickens, described a London square and asked him whether he knew it. Dickens said yes, and how hard the pump was to use. James screamed 'You'll find it harder to pump me,' and slammed the window. John Forster, Dickens's friend, asked a Lunacy Commissioner to examine Lucas. He said there was no sign of insanity; on the contrary, he was a man of profound intellect. Another time, to get an interview Dickens disguised himself as a Scottish Highlander. 'You are an impostor,' screamed Lucas, 'and no gentleman!' When Dickens lampooned him in *Tom Tiddler's Ground* as the loathsome Mr Mopes, Lucas wrote an articulate, incensed letter of complaint to the press.

Lunardi, Vincenzo (1759–1806) Secretary to the Italian Ambassador in London. First* manned flight in Britain was from London to Standon Green* in his 33ft-diameter balloon on 12 September 1784. Montgolfier had made the first flight the year before in a hot-air balloon; Lunardi's was filled with flammable hydrogen. He took off from the Royal Artillery Ground, City Road, London, with a pigeon, cat, dog, food, wine, water and oars to control the balloon. Within minutes he trod on the birdcage and the pigeon flew home. When ice formed on the balloon at Welham Green, he flew low to hand out the half-frozen cat and dog, but the dog refused to leave his master and jumped back in. There is a memorial at Balloon Corner, junction of Huggins, Parsonage and Dellsome lanes. Farm labourers took the cat. The balloon drifted north, rising to 12,000ft before, again because of ice accumulation, he descended two hours and 12 miles later in Standon Green by throwing a grappling hook at a tree. Frightened farmers attacked the balloon with pitchforks. By the time Lunardi had pacified them, friends following him on horseback had caught up and took him to the Bull Inn, Ware, where he dined before staying the night with the MP for Hertford. After a press conference at which he described in detail the first ever aerial view of Britain, he was front-page news. George III asked to meet him, the Prince Regent gave him a commemorative gold watch, women adored him and wore medallions of his portrait. When you read of the hurdles he had to clear to get the balloon in the air it's hard not to admit he earned his fame.

Lutyens, Sir Edwin (1869–1944) Architect. Had famous partnership with garden designer Gertrude Jekyll*. Married Lady Emily Lytton: his father-in-law was Britain's first* Viceroy of India (Lutyens built Viceroy House, New Delhi); his mother-in-law was lady-in-waiting to Queen Victoria. He designed or worked on many properties in

St Martin's Church, Knebworth, designed by Lutyens.

the county, including Temple Dinsley* and the house opposite. Homewood in Knebworth, where the Lutyens children spent their holidays, was built for the Dowager Lady Lytton; in 1973 it became a hotel. He built St Martin's, Knebworth, consecrated by the Bishop of St Albans in 1915 and said by Pevsner to be 'one of Lutyens' most remarkable'. It was extended in 1963 by Sir Albert Richardson. He also built the non-traditional St Mary and St Thomas, Knebworth, which has no church tower and eaves projecting over the walls. Another example of his work is the mansion with huge chimneys built in Langley, near Hitchin, in 1914.

Lytton, Sir Robert 1485: helped Henry Tudor (Henry VII) to defeat Richard III at Bosworth. 1490: bought Knebworth.

Lytton, Sir William 1588: Spanish Armada sighted; beacons lit at Amwell, Gravely and St Albans. Sir William Lytton took command of forces in the county and led them to Tilbury, where Lord Hunsdon* was in command. 1620: built Letchworth Hall. His coat of arms is on the south front.

M

McAdam, John (1756–1836) Highway engineer. Transformed road building the world over. In 1823, when commissioned to improve roads in the county, he moved into Montague House, 68 High Street, Hoddesdon, where he eventually died. His sons gave up their own careers to work with him. He was offered a knighthood but refused. By 1900 most of the main roads in Europe had been Macadamised and the word Tarmac had been coined. Monument in St Augustine's Broxbourne*.

Hoddesdon, once the home of John McAdam.

Macaulay, Lord (1800–59) Historian. Educated at Aspenden Hall, a splendid Tudor house, seat of the Freman family. Sir Ralph Freman also owned Hamels, another Tudor estate near Braughing. Aspenden Hall was demolished and the Freman family died out, leaving the Lordship of Aspenden-Hacon for sale for £2,000. Hamels fared better; it is now East Hertfordshire Golf Club. The 1783 lodges leading to the park, designed by Sir John Soane, have also survived (near Puckeridge roundabout).

Mackenzie, Sir Compton (1883–1972) Author of *Whisky Galore*. Son of actors and brother of actress Fay Compton. 1900: aged 17 moved into the vicarage of Highcross Church near Ware to be coached by the Revd Arnold Overton before taking the Oxford University entrance examination. He joined the Ware Company 1st Volunteers, forerunners of the Territorial Army. He loved the uniform, which cost his father £100. After being recruited by MI6 he became director of the Aegean Intelligence Service and was almost sent to prison for writing about his adventures as a spy.

MacNeice, Louis (1907–63) Poet, radio playwright and broadcaster. With W.H. Auden, Cecil Day-Lewis and Stephen Spender formed the 1930s 'New Poetry' group. He and Betjeman* were at school together and loathed each other. During the war the BBC recruited him for radio propaganda, which he and Orwell dubbed 'The Liar's School'. 1947: in India for BBC reporting on the partition. MacNiece and actress Mary Wimbush bought three cottages in Aldbury, 39, 41 and 43 Stocks Road (knocked together). Louis loved it, the chapel next door and especially The Greyhound pub, where he would sit under the clock. *The Burning Perch* is one of three books written here. In 2000 three of his

The Greyhound pub, Aldbury.

poems were voted *Radio Times* Nation's Favourite Poems of Childhood.

Metroland When the Metropolitan Railway extended to Rickmansworth and Chorleywood, Betjeman's much-loved Metroland was born.

Michael, King of Romania (b. 1921) Mihai I, son of Karol II. 1940: acceded to the throne when his father went into exile. 1947: forced to abdicate after Romania was taken over by Communists. Moved into Ayot House, Ayot St Lawrence*. 2001: Romanian Senate passed law granting him 50 per cent of the president's pay, a residence and a special guard.

Moor Park Open to the public in summer. The famous paintings and historic artefacts are owned by Moor Park Heritage Foundation and the building is owned by Moor Park Golf Course. The original moated manor was built in 1430. Cardinal Wolsey* enlarged it to entertain Henry VIII, Queen Catherine of Aragon and her lady-in-waiting Anne Boleyn. Henry was here with his wife when he began his love affair with Anne. When she stayed here alone, she left behind love letters from Henry, which Wolsey sent to the Pope. Catherine, exiled from court, returned here as a hostage on her way to nearby Ampthill in Bedfordshire. After Wolsey's demise, Henry gave Moor Park to Anne of Cleves. She entertained Henry and Queen Catherine Howard here. 1550: Edward VI gave it to Nicholas Ridley, Bishop of London, but on the accession of Queen Mary he was deposed. Elizabeth I leased it to the Palmer family. In 1610 it was owned first by Henry, Prince of Wales, then, after his early death, by his brother Charles. 1678: James Scott (1649–85), Duke of Monmouth, aka Crofts aka Fitz (= bastard of) Roy (= roi), illegitimate son of Charles II, built a new house. He was executed in 1685. 1720: the present Grade I listed mansion of Portland stone was built in the Palladian style. The interior is by Sir James Thornhill, reluctant father-in-law of his pupil William Hogarth. 1874: Merchant Taylors' School moved in. 1900s: owned by Lord Robert Grosvenor, Duke of Westminster. 1919: William Lever, Lord Leverhulme (d. 1925), of Sunlight Soap, bought the estate. 1937: bought by Rickmansworth UDC. 1944: Operation Market Garden, which resulted in the Battle of Arnhem, was planned here. Some 10,000 men took part in a massive combined air/ground offensive to liberate Holland. 1970s: featured in Betjeman*'s BBC film *Metroland*.

Moore, Henry (1898–1986) Born the seventh child of a miner. His works are in more public places around the world than those of any other sculptor. Official War Artist, famous initially for his Shelter Drawings of Londoners in the underground during the Blitz. His teaching career at Chelsea School of Art ended in 1939 after both it and his London home were bomb damaged. He rented Hoglands, Perry Green, near Much Hadham. After he received £300 for *Reclining Figure*, he bought the 70-acre estate at Perry Green. The Moores remained there for the rest of their lives. 1946: his daughter Mary was born, renewing his interest in the mother and child theme. German Chancellor Helmut Schmidt and French President François Mitterrand both flew to Hoglands to present him with honours. 1972: the Henry Moore Foundation, administered by the Tate Gallery, was formed to prevent his estate from being broken up. It is open to the public on one afternoon every summer under the British Red Cross Open Gardens scheme.

More, Sir Thomas (1477–1535) His father bought Gobions, Little Heath, Brookmans Park and renamed it More Hall. More's *Utopia* is said to have been written here. After More's execution, Henry VIII took Gobions/More Hall. Mary Tudor returned it to the More family; Edward VI took it from them and gave it to Elizabeth I. 1836: Robert Gaussen demolished it. The Folly Gate/Main Gateway (local legend says there is a farthing under each brick) is all that remains. Cared for by English Heritage.

Morrison, Sir Herbert (1888–1965) Labour Cabinet Minister famous for his wartime air-raid shelter, a steel-topped table for families who refused to trek out to the garden to use the Anderson shelter. Leader of LCC during the Second World War, he masterminded the evacuation of school-children from London to the country. Married a girl from Letchworth* when he was sent there in the First World War as a conscientious objector to work on the land at Kidd's Market Gardens. Blind in one eye, he would not anyway have been accepted for active service. Their daughter is the mother of Peter Mandelson. In those days Letchworth was the centre of the underground for conscientious objectors on the run, such as his friend Frederic Osborn, with whom he stayed.

Mosquito Plane 7,781 built. Nicknames: Mossie, the Balsa Bomber, the Wooden Wonder. 1938: de Havilland* proposed an unarmed bomber powered by two Rolls-Royce Merlin engines, faster than any fighter and able to reach Berlin. Realising existing aircraft programmes would need all available metal supplies, he built it from balsa and plywood. A scornful Air Ministry rejected it but had to eat humble pie in 1940. The prototype was built in a hangar disguised as a barn behind Salisbury Hall. Churchill came to see it with Air Ministry officials and in-service bomber crews. The last was withdrawn from RAF photo-reconnaissance units in 1961.

Mosquito Museum De Havilland* Aircraft Heritage Centre, Salisbury Hall, London Colney. Started in 1959 by Walter Goldsmith (owner of the Hall), the de Havilland family and John 'Cat's Eyes' Cunningham. First aircraft museum in Britain; has the prototype of the Mosquito.

Mowlam, Dr Maureen (Mo) (1949–2005) Northern Ireland Secretary. Born in King Street Nursing Home, Watford, one of three children of Tina and Frank Mowlam. Lived at 28 Richmond Drive, a detached house in Cassiobury Park, until the family moved to London when she was 6. Rt Hon. Entered House of Commons 1987 as MP for Redcar. Entered Cabinet as Northern Ireland Secretary after Labour's 1997 election victory. As NI Secretary oversaw the negotiations that led to the 1998 Good Friday Agreement. She was ousted from this job in 1999.

Much Hadham One of the oldest villages in the county, it was a centre of the Roman pottery industry. Country seat of the Bishops of London for 800 years. Here in 1430 began the Tudor* dynasty, when Henry V's widow Catherine (Mrs Owen Tudor) gave birth to Edmund, whose son Henry Tudor took the Crown in battle against Richard III at the Battle of Bosworth Field. The rectory has housed a few radical incumbents. 1515: Thomas Patmore introduced his parishioners to the ideas of Martin Luther, Germany's archprotestant, and allowed his curate to marry. Another rector was Nicholas Ridley, who tried to convert Mary Tudor to Protestantism. After

Mosquito planes at the Aircraft Museum, Salisbury Hall, London Colney.

Elizabethan wall paintings at Forge Cottage, Much Hadham. This detail shows Queen Elizabeth I as King Solomon.

she became Queen she had him burnt at the stake. Although the Bishop's Palace is now separate dwellings, it still has the roof of a fourteenth-century hall, and some brickwork dates from 1650. It has been a school and an asylum. The mother and sister of William Morris lived here for twenty years in the cottage known as Morris Cottage. Henry Moore* lived at nearby Perry Green and is buried at St Thomas's. His 1953 *Heads of a King and Queen* is over the west door of St Andrew's. Inside is his window with the *Tree of Life*. Until 1984 the church was Anglican but is now also Catholic (Church of the Holy Cross).

Much Hadham Forge Four generations of the Page family were blacksmiths here from 1811 to 1980, when Charlie Page retired at the age of 88. His daughter Jean, the last of the family, donated the forge to the Hertfordshire Building Preservation Trust*, which restored the buildings and garden, created a museum of the blacksmith's craft, and employed a working blacksmith. The house contains magnificent and rare sixteenth-century wall paintings (not yet accessible to the public). One shows *The Judgement of Solomon* with Elizabeth I as Solomon. Forge and Museum open Friday, Saturday and Sunday afternoons, April to December.

N

National Gardens Scheme Forty of the county's most beautiful gardens are open to the public under the scheme between March and October every year. Leaflets in libraries.

Naturists If you go down to Bricket Wood* today, you're sure of a big surprise. Spielplatz, Britain's first* residential naturist camp, started in 1929, is still open for business, the only survivor of several in the area at that time. Charles (Mac) and Dorothy Macaskie left their safe, secure, comfortable, boring life in London to buy 10 acres of woodland to live in a tent and rear their daughter Iseult. It became the first Sun Club in Britain. They built chalets, a swimming pool and a road from Lye Lane. In 1961 *Naked, As Nature Intended* was filmed here.

Neckham, Alexander (1157–1217) Scholar, translator of Aesop's* *Fables*. Born on 8 September in St Albans, the same night as Richard I (Lionheart), son of Henry II. Neckham's mother, Richard's wet nurse, reared them as brothers. Neckham was the first Englishman to write about chess, silkworms and the mariner's compass. His first studies were in the Abbey School, St Albans, where he became a teacher. He was a prolific writer, and his works are in the British Library.

Nellie Dean The mill where she used to sit and dream is said to be in Lemsford. There never was a Nellie Dean and no one knows who wrote the song made popular by Gertie

Britain's first naturist camp.

Gitana, who entertained First World War soldiers. There are four claims as to the song's writer: (i) J.P. Skelly in 1881, when he was staying at nearby Brocket Hall, (ii) Boer War soldiers, (iii) First World War soldiers stationed in Lemsford, (iv) Henry W. Armstrong, an American.

New River Not a river, but an artificial water supply for London. 1600: a question was asked in Parliament about the crisis in the lack of clean drinking water. A man called Ingelbert put forward a plan to bring water from Am Well and Chad Well via a brick vault. Another, Colthurst, submitted a proposal for an open trench. 1604: Act of Parliament to bring water from Great Amwell questioned in the House by outraged MP for Hertfordshire. 1606: Act of Parliament authorised Colthurst to bring in water via his trench. 1607: second Act allowed Ingelbert to bring in water via a brick vault. 1613: the New River, hand cut, 38 miles long (half the length is in the county), 4ft deep, 10ft wide and 60ft above sea level, was completed by Colthurst's ex-business partner, Sir Hugh Myddleton. Thames Water engineers say they couldn't improve on the scheme today. 112ft higher at its source than where the river ends in Islington, the water follows the 100ft contour line. The drop of 5in per mile meant the water flowed slowly through Broxbourne, Cheshunt, Enfield, Wood Green, Hornsey, Haringey, Holloway and Islington. Some 150 bridges were built along the route. In some places the river was an aqueduct.

New Towns Hertfordshire has three New Towns. Stevenage (1946), Hatfield (1948) and Hemel Hempstead (1950). Letchworth and Welwyn, although new towns, are not New Towns, but Garden Cities*, built long before the New Towns Act, which was passed to relieve London's chronic post-war housing problem. Industrial development was incorporated into the plans so that they did not end up as dormitory suburbs of the capital. Viscount Esher was the architect for Hatfield. His father was a close friend of Edward VII, George V and Edwin Lutyens*. He built three shopping centres, a church and high-rise housing with concrete walls and aluminium roofs. When a storm blew the roofs off high rises and water got into his community centre, ruining the insulation, Esher's practice suffered.

New Towns Act 1946 With 27,600 London homes uninhabitable because of the Blitz, the Act was implemented first in Hertfordshire. The decentralisation of towns surrounded by a green belt, recommended by Ebenezer Howard fifty years previously, was fundamental to post-war government planning policy. The towns made a great impact on the county. In 1943 the population was 552,410; thirty years later it was almost double and the environment was radically changed. Stevenage was the first* site because of its proximity to the A1 and excellent rail service. Hemel Hempstead, with good access to the M1, expanded its population from 21,000 to 60,000. Hatfield's population increased from 9,000 to 22,000. All are functional, but were and are considered sterile by some.

Nuthampstead Second World War American Air Force base for B-17 'Flying Fortress' bombers. Americans often visit the memorial outside the Woodman pub. Locals ducked instinctively as the bombers skimmed the roofs of their thatched cottages. 1959: airfield closed. 1968–70: Roskill Commission considered it as one of four possible sites for a third London Airport.

Odhams Press Watford. 1906: *John Bull*. 1920s: the *People, Daily Herald, Woman's Own*. 1930s: *Picture Post, Woman*. 1954: moved to new headquarters in St Albans Road. Odhams had the largest Press Hall in Europe with the most up-to-date equipment available. It employed 2,000 people, operating twenty-four hours and producing six million magazines a week. 1960: *TV Times*. 1969: Associated-Iliffe Press, Newnes and Odhams merged to become IPC (International Publishing Corporation), owner of *Daily Mirror, People* and *Sun*. 1970: IPC acquired by Reed. 1982: Robert Maxwell bought Odhams with 23 acres of land and existing print order worth £30 million for knock-down price of £1.5 million. He sacked half the staff and transferred the rest to Sun Printers. Odhams-Sun became part of Maxwell Communications Corp. 1998: Cinven bought IPC from Reed for £860 million. 2001: US group Time Inc bought IPC from Cinven for £1.15 billion. 2003: Odhams, with its long history, disappeared.

Offa Anglo-Saxon King of Mercia who built the famous Dyke. 757: marshalled his forces at Hitchin*. Defeated Beornred in battles for Mercia at Pirton, Pegsdon and at what is now Offley, where he built a palace. 792: founded Benedictine monastery in Hitchin (site of St Mary's). 793: founded St Albans monastery and gave The Bury, Rickmansworth, to St Albans to house the shire reeve (sheriff). He also gave the area round the Stort to the Bishops of London. 795: died at Offley. Some sources say he was buried near the Ouse at Bedford, others in St Mary's, Hitchin. 1923: silver coin found on a footpath between Hitchin and Offley bearing inscription OFFA/REX.

Old Moore's Almanack Contrary to popular legend, Henry Andrews (1743–1820) of Royston did not start the publication. It began in 1697 with Dr Francis Moore, a physician at the court of Charles II. Henry was compiler of the Royal Almanack. He was also Calculator for the Nautical Almanack. Andrews, an astronomer who lived on the corner of High Street and George Lane, seems to have been a jack-of-all-trades and master of all. He opened a boarding school on Fish Hill, where he taught maths and astronomy, and a shop in Melbourn Street, where he sold barometers, thermometers and mathematical instruments. In 1776, after Dr Hutton, editor of Old Moore's Almanack, invited Henry to be his assistant, annual sales rocketed to 500,000. However, during the forty-three years he worked on the Almanack Andrews had no pay rise. His salary remained £25 p.a.. He is buried in Royston.

Olivier, Sir Laurence (1907–89) Actor. Spent his boyhood in Letchworth, where he made his acting debut. His father, the Revd Gerard Olivier, was rector of St Mary's, old Letchworth. The Queen Anne house where they lived is now owned by St Christopher's School. He sang in the choir at St Mary's, and was a shepherd in the nativity play in St George's Church Hall, Norton Way. After his adored mother died of a brain tumour, the family moved to a new rectory in Pixmore Way, which served St Michael and All Angels, Norton Way South (demolished in 1967). 1924: his father moved again just before Olivier got his first paid acting job in St Christopher School theatre.

Orchards Once common. Rivers of Sawbridgeworth closed in 1985. Stones of

The Old Rectory, Letchworth, the boyhood home of Sir Laurence Olivier.

Croxley Green is still there. Tewin Orchard, Welwyn, is a nature reserve open to the public. The Brownlees, a russet apple popular for its cerise-pink blossom, was introduced by William Brownlees, a nurseryman in Hemel Hempstead in 1848. The Golden Reinette apple grows best in this county. Lane's Prince Albert apple was raised by Thomas Squire of Berkhamsted and named by John Lane when he started to produce it commercially. It became popular as it keeps its shape when cooked. The original tree was still in a High Street garden in 1936.

Ovaltine 1913: factory opened in King's Langley with 11 employees (grew to 1,400). At the ultra-modern dairy and poultry farm, 450 acres were given over to prize-winning Jersey cows, 50,000 chickens and barley. 1935: Radio Luxembourg Ovaltiney Club had five million members: 'We are the Ovaltineys, little girls and boys'. Ovaltine was the official sports drink for many years at the Olympics. Sir Edmund Hillary took it up Mount Everest in 1953; Freya Stark took it on her travels across the Arabian Desert; John Betjeman mentioned it in his poems. It was issued to soldiers in tablet form during the Second World War. 2002: factory closed; site now owned by Renewable Energy Systems (see Wind Turbine*).

P

Panshanger Gothic mansion, home of the Cowper family for 200 years. John Buchan* spent holidays here with Bron Herbert, fellow-student at Oxford, nephew and heir of Lord Cowper. The last owner, Lord Desborough, sold it in 1953 to a gravel company, which demolished it.

Panshanger Oak The 80ft tree at Panshanger Park, Hertingfordbury, is on the Tree Council's conservation list. Believed to have been planted by Elizabeth I, it was one of fifty Great British Trees chosen to mark the Golden Jubilee of Elizabeth II. Known to be over 500 years old, this tree, the largest maiden (non-pollarded) oak in Britain, is 42ft in circumference.

Paris, Matthew (1200–59) Medieval historian. Became novice monk at St Albans Abbey at the age of 17. Succeeded Roger of Wendover* as official chronicler of the Abbey. Wrote *Major Chronicles from The Creation* and biographies of St Alban, Edward the Confessor and Thomas Becket. Admired by Henry III, who often visited him.

Parish Records Date from 1539, when Henry VIII decreed every parish must record weekly details of baptisms, marriages and burials. Housed in County Record Office, Hertford.

The Great Oak, Panshanger.

Peasants' Revolt 14 June 1381: men in St Albans* and Watford* were ordered to join the London uprising or their towns would be burnt. After Wat Tyler was killed in a fight with the Mayor of London, Richard II* arrived in St Albans with a thousand men and ordered that Father John Ball, one of Wat's right-hand men, be executed in front of him. He then had the insurgents brought from Hertford gaol and executed. All men over 15 years of age resident in the county were assembled in the abbey and were made to swear to be his faithful subjects.

Pelhams Three villages once owned by the Furneux (Furnix) family. Furneux Pelham church has stained glass by William Morris and Burne-Jones. St Mary the Virgin, Brent (Burnt) Pelham, has a giant called Piers under a thirteenth-century black marble slab in the north wall. Lord of the manor, he is said to have slain a dragon owned by the devil who vowed to have his soul whether he was buried in or outside the church. In choosing the wall Piers cheated the devil. Stocking Pelham has a little church and a barn twice as big. The church, which has been here 600 years, has a bell, said to have rung out the news of Agincourt. Outside are stocks, one of only two sets left in the county. The other is at Aldbury*.

Penn, William (1644–1716) Founded Pennsylvania. 1672: married Guilelma Springett at King John's Farm, Shepherds Lane, Chorleywood* (first son named Springett). They moved into Basing House, High Street, Rickmansworth* (plaque) and stayed until the lease expired in December 1676. A close friend of founder of the Quakers, George Fox*, who stayed with him at Basing House, he dreamed of founding a colony in America where Friends could worship

Basing House, Rickmansworth.

without persecution. Pennsylvania was named after his father, Admiral Sir William Penn. William Jnr wanted 'New Wales' (he was Welsh) or 'Sylvania', but Charles II insisted on 'Penn Sylvania' because Admiral Penn had lent him money (repaid with a hefty chunk of the New World). He is buried at the Friends' Meeting House, Jordan, near Rickmansworth. The present Basing House (museum) was built in 1740. It is possible Penn's house was incorporated into the design.

People Power (selection) 1737: *John Wilkes* (1727–97) politician, MP, educated at Richard Hale School, Hertford; fought to abolish the practice of press-ganging men into the armed forces; introduced concept of 'no taxation without representation', which spread to America; won freedom of the press to publish debates in the House of Commons; started Bill of Rights Society to abolish rotten boroughs and allow working men to share in the power to make laws. 1866: *Augustus Smith* removed railings erected around Berkhamsted common by Lord Brownlow. 1960s: *Tony Rook* saved a Roman bath* at Welwyn for the nation. 1972: *Violet Rowe* (1910–2001) formed the Amwell House Preservation Society when the County Council decided to raze John Scott's* irreplaceable eighteenth-century architectural gem, and saved it. 1980s: *Jill Grey* got the British School, Hitchin listed; *Brian Limbrick* overturned its sale, *volunteers* keep it running. In 2002 it was granted Registered Museum status. 1988: *James Hannaway et al.* saved the Rex Cinema, Berkhamsted, from demolition; it reopened for business in 2004. 1989: *Friends of Forster Country* formed 'To preserve for all time the open green space to the north of Stevenage which is known as The Forster Country'. 1990: *Friends of Rivers Nursery*, Sawbridgeworth, brought it back into production.

2000: *David Farmer* is trying to save Panshanger. 2005: *Tring locals* refused to let Dacorum Council raze the cattle market office. Wanting it for a museum, they demanded a public inquiry and won.

Pepys, Samuel (1633–1703) Diarist and Royal Navy reformer. At aged 27 started a diary in a code based on a new form of shorthand (tachygraphy) invented by Thomas Shelton (stopped when he was 36). Following the publication of the hugely successful Evelyn* (close friend of Pepys) diaries, John Smith* was given the task of cracking the code. They were published after years of painstaking deciphering of a highly idiosyncratic mixture of shorthand and foreign languages. Pepys travelled all over the county and knew it well. His diary mentions Baldock, Barkway, Barnet, Biggleswade, Bishop's Stortford, Buntingford, Hatfield, Puckeridge, Stevenage, Ware, and Welwyn.

Perrers, Alice (d. 1400) High-born daughter of a Hertfordshire knight, she married William de Windsor and became lady-in-waiting to Queen Philippa, wife of Edward III. 1369: after Philippa's death she became Edward's mistress and he fell under her influence. 1375: Edward gave her the manors of Hitchin and Wendover. By now he was senile, so Alice, with his son, John of Gaunt, ruled England. 1376: when Edward died, she was alone in the room with him and stole rings from his fingers, for which she was banished by Parliament.

Peter the Wild Boy (1713–85). Died at Broadway Farm, Northchurch, Berkhamsted. He is buried in the churchyard near the porch. Inside is a dedication brass. In 1725, aged 12, he was found in woods near Hanover, Germany. He walked on all fours, ran up trees like a squirrel and ate grass. The Elector of Hanover (King George I of

England) took him to amuse the London court. Daniel Defoe* and Jonathan Swift both wrote about him; Dickens put him in *Edwin Drood*. He was sent to Mr and Mrs Fenn of Haxters End Farm, near Bourne End, who were paid to care for him. He wore a collar bearing his address. Haxters End Lane was renamed Little Heath Lane following the demolition of the farmhouse.

Pevsner, Sir Nikolaus (1902–83) Architectural historian. In *The Buildings of England: Hertfordshire* (1953, 1977), said the county is 'uneventful but lovable'. Toured in a 1933 Wolseley Hornet borrowed from his publisher (Penguin). Wrote: 'Ashwell has more architecturally worthwhile houses than any other [village] in the county'; 'Hitchin is after St Albans, the most visually satisfying town in the county'; 'Bayfordbury grounds are beautiful'; 'Balls Park is one of the most puzzling houses of Hertfordshire. Although it appears to be early Georgian in fact dates from around 1640'; 'Stanstead Bury has an eminently picturesque exterior . . . delight the eye of any painter'; 'Gilston is a large asymmetrical mansion of random rubble in the Early Tudor style with Gothic details'; Pishiobury is 'mildly medievalizing'; praised the 1938 Bauhaus-influenced Roche building on Broadwater Road, Welwyn Garden City: Barclay School, Stevenage; 'no façade, indeed no face, yet not at all in any derogatory sense'.

Picture Post **Magazine** Sun Printers, Watford, pioneered colour printing in 1914. The company was commissioned by the government to produce forgery-proof banknotes following the recall of gold coins. 1934: pioneered gravure colour printing. Commissioned to print *Picture Post* for Odhams. The magazine, which introduced photojournalism, within four months was selling 1,350,000 copies a week. 1940s: Sun Printers produced secret maps for the 1944 D-Day invasion. 1949: magazine

was selling 1,422,000 a week. 1957: after internal disputes magazine closed. 1986: Robert Maxwell merged it with Odhams* as Odhams-Sun.

Pishiobury 1510: John Chauncy tried unsuccessfully to buy this lovely Tudor mansion. Later it was given by Henry VIII to Anne Boleyn. After he had her executed, he rented it to the Chauncys. There was friction between Lord Hunsdon, a favourite of Elizabeth I, and Henry Chauncy, who refused to sell him Gilston*, so Hunsdon persuaded her to cancel the lease. Homeless, Henry Chauncy began building a house on his estate in 1550. He called it New Place. Its entrance porch is still in the garden of Gilston Park. In a niche above the door is a bust of Elizabeth I dated 1585.

Potter, Beatrix (1866–1943) Writer and artist. Said of *The Tale of Peter Rabbit*: 'The potting shed and the actual geraniums in Mr McGregor's garden were in Hertfordshire.' From birth until age 25, when her grand-mother died at 91 and the house was sold, she spent every summer at Camfield Place, Essendon, a 300-acre estate laid out by Capability Brown. In 1892 when her grandmother was dying she stayed at Bedwell Park, Essendon. In her secret, coded journal she wrote: 'The place I love best in the world is Camfield Place.' She painted a watercolour of Mill Green Watermill, Hatfield (now a museum), called *A Hertfordshire Farm*.

Potters Bar Will for a long time be associated with the 2002 rail* disaster. Canada Life is the main employer (900). Nearby Wrotham (pronounced Root-ham) Park, a magnificent mansion, was designed for the ill-fated Admiral Byng in 1754. He was sent to prevent the French taking British-owned Minorca but failed and so was court-martialled and shot. It is still owned by the same family; Robert Byng runs the estate. A favourite venue for film-makers, this is where *Gosford Park* was filmed. The famous Dame Alice Owen School in Potters Bar, originally based in the London borough of Islington, was founded in 1603 when James I granted her a licence to open a Free Grammar School to 'teach the sons and daughters of the poor abiding in Islington, Isledon and Clerkenwell'. Dame Alice is buried in St Mary's, Islington. 1977: after 363 years at the Angel, Islington, the school moved to Potters Bar following orders from the Greater London Council (GLC), Inner London Education Authority and Islington Council to become comprehensive or move. Many Islingtonians were so keen for their children to attend that they also moved there.

Prime Ministers *Robert Cecil* (1563–1612) of Hatfield House*, MP for Hertfordshire. England's first PM (to Elizabeth I*). *William Lamb* (1779–1848) of Brocket Hall*, husband of the infamous Lady Caroline Lamb*, became Viscount Melbourne, PM to William IV and to the 18-year-old Queen Victoria. *Lord Palmerston* (1748–1865) of Brocket Hall (via his wife) was three times PM to Queen Victoria. *Robert Cecil* (1830–1903), three times PM to Queen Victoria, was her favourite. He died at Hatfield House and was buried in the grounds. He said: 'English policy is to float lazily downstream occasionally putting out a diplomatic boathook to avoid collisions.'

Profumo, John (b. 1915) Centre of the biggest scandal to hit British politics in the twentieth century. During mass media frenzy he hid in the Dower House, Mandeville Road, Westmill. The War Minister's 1963 affair with prostitute Christine Keeler, who was sleeping with Ivanov, a Russian master spy, at the same time, led to the downfall of the Conservative government.

Puckeridge On the main road from London to Cambridge. Much loved by Charles Lamb* and Samuel Pepys*, whose diaries mention the town, including the Crown and Falcon and Thorpe House, sixteen times. Until recently it was famous for its hunt*, the last in the county.

Purdom, C.B. Writer. Financial director of Welwyn Garden City (WGC) Ltd; wrote *The Garden City*, *The Building of Satellite Towns*. Passionate about theatre, he put on WGC's first play in 1920 in Brick Wall Barn, Shaw's *The Showing Up of Blanco Posnet*. The next year he founded WGC Theatre Society and produced Shaw's *Candida*. He wrote *A Guide to the Plays of Bernard Shaw* (1963). His passion for theatre was inherited by his son, the actor Edmund Purdom (b. 1924–), who found fame in Hollywood in 1954 in *The Student Prince*, co-starring Ann Blyth. Edmund also played the leading role in *The Egyptian*. He lives in Rome.

Quenells Of Berkhamsted*. Marjorie and Charles wrote educational textbooks, their son Peter wrote biographies (Shakespeare, Boswell, Byron, Ruskin *et al.*). He attended school with Graham Greene* and Claud Cockburn*. Together they read forbidden books, e.g. Oscar Wilde's *The Yellow Book* and *Madame Bovary*, on Berkhamsted Common.

R

Radlett The famous Elstree Murder of 1823 was in fact the Radlett murder (the victim was dumped in Elstree). John Thurtell, a wealthy gambler, had a grudge against fellow-gambler William Weare, a solicitor, whom he said had cheated him of £300 at cards. He invited him to spend a weekend gambling at William Probert's cottage in Gills Hill Lane (still called Murder Lane). They travelled from London in Thurtell's gig on 24 October 1823. As they neared the Wagon and Horses, Watling Street, Thurtell shot Weare. The bullet glanced off his cheekbone so Thurtell slit his throat. Probert and another gambling friend, Hunt, dumped Weare in Elstree. When the gun and knife were found near the cottage, Probert turned King's Evidence. The inquest was held in the Artichoke pub, Elstree Hill North. When Thurtell and Hunt came up before William Lamb (later Lord Melbourne) at the Hertford Assizes, Thurtell was charged with murder, Hunt with being an accessory. A gallows was built during the trial. They were sentenced to death and Thurtell's body was ordered to be anatomised. Hunt's sentence was commuted to transportation and he was shipped to Botany Bay. Thirty-year-old Thurtell dressed for his execution on 9 January 1824 in a brown greatcoat with a black velvet collar, breeches, gaiters and a waistcoat with gold buttons. Plays and ballads were written about the murder, which caught the imagination of many writers, including Scott*, Dickens* and Bulwer-Lytton*. 1929:

Handley Page* opened an aerodrome in Colney Street. Production focused on the most famous of all wartime bombers, the Halifax, with Rolls-Royce engines. It was officially named by Lord Halifax at Radlett. 25 October 1939: first flight.

Rail Disasters The county has 60,000 daily rail commuters. 8 August 1996: 1 person killed, 69 injured, when a train collided with a stationary train at Watford South. 17 October 2000: 4 people killed, 35 injured, when the GNER London–Leeds train derailed at Hatfield. 10 May 2002: 7 people died, 70 injured, when the London–King's Lynn train crashed at Potters Bar. Three of the four carriages were derailed and one ploughed along the platform and smashed into Darkes Lane bridge.

Read, Sir Herbert (1893–1968) Art historian. Captain in the First World War. DSO, MC. Advocate of modern art, his recognition of the importance of artists such as Henry Moore* placed British art in a world context. Founded the ICA, London. Like Moore, moved from London to Much Hadham during the war. He tried to persuade his friend Piet Mondrian to join them, but he refused. Wrote his famous book *Education through Art* while here.

Redbourn Site of twelfth-century priory dedicated to St Amphibalus, whose life was reputedly saved by Alban*. Princess Elizabeth, taken ill on her way to court in 1554 to answer charges of treason, stayed here. The village is said to have the oldest cricket team in the county (1666). 1822: William Cobbett* loved this place. Before the railways, eighty coaches a day passed through. Local GP Dr Henry Stephens (1796–1864), whose father was landlord of the Bull, studied with John Keats at Barts and shared lodgings with him. Stephens invented ink for 'reservoir pens' (later called fountain pens) 'a blue black writing fluid – writes blue dries black'. Because it was permanent, it was made mandatory for legal documents and ships' logbooks. Redbournbury Mill, in use until the 1960s, has been restored to working order and is open to visitors. The County Show is held here every summer.

Rhodes, Cecil (1853–1902) Imperialist. Endowed Rhodes Oxford Scholarships for students from the colonies, USA and Germany. Seventh child of the Revd Francis Rhodes, vicar of St Michael's, Bishop's Stortford. Born Stratford House (now a museum). Attended local grammar school. Rhodesia was named after him. Went to South Africa at age 17 to join his brother. 1871: involved in the early development of the Kimberley diamond mine. 1880: later formed the De Beers Mining Company. Died aged 49, leaving instructions he was to be buried with African chiefs in the Matopopo hills.

Richard I Lionheart (1157–99) Born 8 September, the same night as Alexander Neckham* of St Albans, whose mother was his wet nurse. Richard preferred crusading to ruling. Forced to marry, he chose the Spanish princess Berengaria of Navarre, and gave her Berkhamsted Castle. Although Queen of England, she never set foot in the country.

Richard II (1367–1400) Only child of Edward, the Black Prince, and Joan of Kent. This is the Boy King who stood up to Wat Tyler in the Peasants' Revolt, who, like his grandfather, Edward II, was homosexual and like his grandfather was murdered. 1376: his father died at Berkhamsted. 1381: the Peasants' Revolt*. 1393: held court at King's Langley and spent Christmas there. 1395: at Langley for Christmas. 1396: at Langley when his uncle, John of Gaunt, arrived to ask the King's permission to marry his mistress, Katherine Swynford. The honeymooners stayed at Hertford Castle. 1399: Richard gave Hertford Castle to Edmund, Duke of York. 31 August: Richard held at St Albans before being taken to the Tower. Henry of Bolingbroke proclaimed himself king and took the throne as Henry IV. 1400: after his murder at Pontefract and last rites held in secret in St Paul's, he was secretly buried at King's Langley. Fourteen years later Henry V had his remains placed in the Confessor's chapel, Westminster Abbey. Act III Scene iv of Shakespeare's *Richard II* is set in Langley Palace.

Richard III (1452–85) 1484: gave the manor of Cheshunt to Walter Devereux, Lord Ferrers. 1486: took Hertford Castle from Elizabeth Woodville and gave it to her daughter, Elizabeth of York.

Rickmansworth See George Eliot*, William Penn*. Charles I sold the manor to Sir Thomas Fotherley. The family became extinct when the last member died in the 1694 earthquake in Jamaica. St Mary's Church, rebuilt in the 1850s, is said to have a window from St John's in Rouen, removed during the French Revolution. The Crucifixion window is by Burne-Jones.

Rivers *Ash*: tributary of the Lea* (joins near Ware). *Beane*: rises near Cromer. *Chess*: source at Chesham, ends at Wendover. On its banks are a Roman watermill, watercress beds, a trout farm and a tropical fish-breeding farm. *Colne*: runs through North Mimms, Watford, and Rickmansworth. Receives the Ver, Bulborne and Chess. *Gade*: rises in Gaddesden, joins the Colne near Rickmansworth. Boreholes were sunk to serve the new town of Hemel Hempstead. *Hiz*: a tributary of the Ivel; source is in Charlton. The Oughton and Purwell run through Hitchin and join to form the Hiz.

Ivel: runs through Stevenage, Graveley, Baldock into Bedfordshire to join the Great Ouse. Lea*: see separate entry. *Mimram*: joins the Lea near Hertford. *Rib*: source near Buntingford; joins the Lea between Hertford and Ware. *Stort*: named after Bishop's Stortford. It joins the Lea at the county boundary between Hertfordshire and Essex. *Ver*: rises near Markyate, runs south-south-east to St Albans, then south until it joins the Colne.

Roads The oldest is the Icknield Way*. Hertfordshire has more Roman roads than any other county in the UK. The major roads are *Ermine Street* (A10 London to York), Old North Road. The original Roman surface can be walked on between Cheshunt and Ware; *Watling Street* (A5 London to Wroxeter via St Albans); *Akemen Street* (A41 London to Cirencester); *Stane Street* (east–west between St Albans and Colchester). Why did they fall into disrepair? We didn't need them; they were built for the army. Those we used led to other villages and until it was ordered that signposts be put up, travellers hired local guides. 1637: first* weekly stage-coach, London–St Albans. 1663: trusts set up to mend, improve, lay, align and ease gradient. Toll-gates (turnpikes) were built to collect tolls. The first* was at Wadesmill. The road was closed with a spiked bar to prevent riders jumping over. 1697: JPs ordered to erect signposts. 1744: JPs ordered to erect milestones. 1750–1800: main roads were Macadamised. 1784: first mail coach. 1835: Highways Act; parishes had to look after roads on their patch. 1838: railways came as roads were improving. 1860s: turnpikes taken down. 1894: rural district councils responsible for road repair. 1920: Ministry of Transport established. 1930s: county councils set up, responsible for road maintenance in the counties. 1936: repair of trunk roads taken over by Ministry of Transport. 1960s: beginning of motorways – first planned road system since Roman times.

Roman Bath (AD 250) Discovered at Welwyn by local archaeologist Tony Rook. Preserved in a steel vault 30ft below the A1M (A1000, Junction 6). In 1960, walking near his home Mr Rook spotted a tile poking out the bank of the Mimram and discovered the bath of a third-century Roman house. Excavation was a race against time because the A1M was being built.

Romans Numerous artefacts on display in museums all over the county. 1847: Roman theatre discovered at St Albans. It was later filled in, and uncovered again in the 1930s. One of only two in Britain (the other is at Caerleon, South Wales) 2003: third-century 15cm-high silver figurine of a Roman goddess discovered near Baldock by a metal detectorist, a find of international importance.

Romanov, Mikhail Alexandrovitch (1878–1918) Grand Duke. 1913: Michael, brother of Russian Tsar Nicholas II, had an affair with the twice-divorced lady-in-waiting to his sister. A child was born, her husband divorced her and they contracted a morganatic marriage. Michael was deprived of the regency and exiled; the couple decided to live in England and rented Knebworth House. March 1917: the Tsar was forced to abdicate in favour of Michael, who was known for a very short time as Michael II but never reigned and is not counted as a Tsar. He was murdered on 12 June 1917 by the Bolsheviks, who floated rumours of his execution to test the reaction of his cousin George V. His silence and that of David Lloyd George opened the way for them to murder Nicholas II and his family on 17 July. 1952: Michael's wife died in exile.

Roses Although Wilfred Harkness, landlord, Raven Inn, Hexton, in the 1900s had a passion for growing roses, contrary to legend the famous Harkness Rose did not start with him. The company started in 1879 in Yorkshire. Jack Harkness started growing roses in Hitchin in 1959. Among many commemorative blooms is the 2003 Soham Rose. Profits from its sale go to the Holly and Jessica Memorial Fund. Also launched the Princess Diana Rose and 'Mummy' (the young Princes' tribute on their wreath). A £20m Memorial Rose Garden for Princess Diana proposed in 2001 and intended to be the largest in the world filled with the commemorative 'England's Rose' never materialised.

Rose's Lime Juice Britain's first branded fruit juice. 1947: bombed out of London, the bottling plant moved to Boxmoor Wharf. Unprocessed lime juice in oak vats was transported from London docks to Boxmoor by barge along the Grand Union Canal. The clear green juice was drawn off, filtered, sweetened and bottled. The Rose family was friendly with Mr Dubonnet, so the drink of that name also came here for bottling. 1964: the wharf featured in *The Bargee* with Eric Sykes and Harry H. Corbett. 1981: Roses taken over by Schweppes; Boxmoor works closed.

Rothschild Lionel was finally allowed to take his seat in the House of Commons in 1858, eleven years after his election (until then Jews not allowed to be MPs). Lionel bought Tring Manor* as a wedding present for his son Nathan. 1868: birth of Nathan's son, Walter, of Zoological* Museum fame. 1885: Nathan created Lord Rothschild, the first Jewish peer.

Roundabouts Britain's first was Sollershott in Letchworth Garden City* (1908). It has been featured on BBC's *Top Gear* and in many motoring magazines. In 2005 appeared

Britain's first roundabout, Letchworth Garden City.

on a roundabout calendar that, initially produced as a joke, became a best-seller. Another famous roundabout is in Hemel Hempstead, dubbed the Magic Roundabout because drivers can go round in either direction. In 1973 the road around the roundabout was made into two lanes. The inside lane runs anticlockwise, the outside lane clockwise. In the 1990s experts suggested that traffic lights should replace it, but a Save Our Roundabout campaign won the day.

Royal Veterinary College Unique in Europe, the first* and largest veterinary training school in the UK was opened in North Mymms in 1959. 1982: Sefton Hospital named after the cavalry horse that sustained terrible injuries in a 1982 IRA bombing in London in which seven horses died.

Royston The Royse Stone, a 2-ton boulder, once the base of a crucifix, is at Market Cross in the town centre. James I* had a hunting lodge in Kneesworth Street. He was here when told about the Gunpowder Plot*. It was also here that he signed Walter Raleigh's death warrant to, so it's said, appease the Spanish Ambassador. The famous Royston Cave (cavern to be precise: caves are natural formations; this is man-made), discovered in 1742 under Melbourn Street, is a phenomenon. There is only one similar in the world, in the Czech Republic. Bottle-shaped, with medieval wall carvings of religious figures from the Old and New Testaments, saints and symbols, the structure possibly dates back to 3000 BC.

Rushden The church has a monument to Sir Adolphus Meetkerke, brought here in 1754 from St Botolph's, Aldersgate. Flemish Ambassador to the court of Elizabeth I, it was he who built Julians, the manor house. Trollope fans the world over have probably heard of Julians. The family did not, as it expected, inherit the manor, and instead lived in poverty until Fanny managed to get a book published. If Anthony's father Thomas had become the squire, would Anthony have written his wonderful stories? Because the drive was directly opposite the Moon and Stars pub and very public, the squire who foiled the Trollope plans by secretly courting a Baldock woman built a new one so that he could come and go without being seen. Julians is still lived in.

Ryder, Sam (1858–1936) Seed merchant, founder of the Ryder Cup. Ryder was the first to package seeds and sell them by mail order. He married a girl from Bishop's Stortford. They lived in Folly Lane, St Albans, and started selling penny packets – orchids or mustard and cress, all the same price. Husband and wife sorted seeds, prepared catalogues and filled packets in the garden shed. They became so successful that they

Wall carvings in Royston Cave.

bought Marlborough House (now Loreto RC Girls' School) and built a headquarters on Holywell Hill, opening the Seed Hall (Café Rouge) where customers could view the plants. At 50, when Ryder suffered a breakdown owing to overwork, his doctor suggested he take up golf, so he joined Verulam Golf Club. 1926: he visited Wentworth for a pre-Open qualifying tournament and got American and British golfers together in a friendly competition. The prize was £5 for the winning team, with chicken sandwiches and champagne. The Ryder Cup was born. 1927: the first Ryder Cup match. He donated the Mappin and Webb gold cup, cost £250; his mentor and coach Abe Mitchell was used as a model for the figure on the lid of the cup. Died January 1936 and buried in Hatfield Road Cemetery, St Albans. A mashie was buried with him. Ryder's Seeds closed in the 1960s.

Ryder, Sue (1923–2000) Lady Ryder of Warsaw. Married Leonard Cheshire*. During the war she met people of superhuman courage and saw suffering on such a scale that in 1953 she established the Sue Ryder Foundation to commemorate them. Her determination spanned five decades of astonishing achievements and transformed the lives of hundreds of thousands. Hers is also the story of Fanys and Bods: FANYs (First Aid Nursing Yeomanry) supported 'bods' (secret agents). She undertook her initial Special Operations Executive* training at Special Training School (STS) 17, Hertford, then transferred to Station 18, Frogmore Watton, at Stone, where bods, supposed allied officers, supposedly convalesced. Sue Ryder called her Homes' residents Bods in their honour.

Rye House Plot 1443: licence granted to Sir Andrew Ogard to 'impark and fortify the Maner of Rye'. 1583: moated castle built. The gatehouse is the oldest brick building in the county. 1683: owner Richard Rumbold, Lord Shaftesbury, the Earl of Essex and the Earl of Bedford openly declared their hatred of Charles II and his brother James. There were many plots to kill Charles and James, but the Rye House Plot was considered the most likely to succeed. The narrow lane outside the castle was to be blocked by an overturned cart, a common enough sight; 100 armed men in the grounds would shoot the royal brothers and finish them off by sword. The planned date for the attack, on their return journey from Newmarket, was 1 April, but on 22 March a fire burnt down half the town. Charles and James helped with fire-fighting before returning to London. Rumbold, Shaftesbury and Bedford were executed. Arthur, Earl of Essex, Lord Lieutenant of Hertfordshire, was taken from his home, Cassiobury, to the Tower, where he committed suicide. Lesser plotters were hanged outside the Rye House Inn opposite the castle. There is a permanent exhibition in the Gatehouse.

S

St Albans This is where Cassivellaunus* relocated after Julius Caesar demolished his headquarters at Wheathampstead. By AD 50 the county's oldest town was the third largest in Roman Britain, called Verulamium (from the River Ver). AD 209: Alban* martyred. 793: town renamed when Offa* built a monastery dedicated to Alban. 1381: Peasants' Revolt*. Fifteenth century: Battles* of St Albans. 1539: Abbey dissolved by Henry VIII. 1553: Edward VI sold the remains to the town for £400. 1643: headquarters of Earl of Essex's Parliamentarian Army. The High Sheriff of Hertfordshire was arrested by Cromwell after he read a Royal Proclamation from the steps of the Eleanor Cross. 1877: Letters Patent granting the Abbey cathedral status and the town a city charter. Less than a tenth of the city has been excavated. Local legend has it the daughter of Mary Walsh, a plumber's daughter, and her husband Mr Carpenter, both from St Albans, married into the Strathmore aristocracy (Bowes-Lyon*).

St Ippollitts Spelling is arbitrary on road signs. 1087: founded by Judith, niece of William I, Prioress of Elstow Abbey, Bedfordshire, this Norman church is dedicated to Hippolytus, patron saint of horses; one of only two in the UK dedicated to him, the other being in Dorset.

St Paul's Waldenbury Childhood home of Elizabeth, the Queen Mother*. Gardens sometimes open to the public in summer. 1720s: bought by Edward Gilbert (coat of arms in the church). His daughter Mary married a Bowes and their son George married Eleanor Verney in 1724. Their daughter Mary Bowes (b. 1749), Edward Gilbert's only grandchild, married John Lyon, 9th Earl of Strathmore.

Salisbury Hall London Colney. 1380: built by Sir John Montague, Earl of Salisbury. Alice, Countess of Salisbury, married Sir Richard Neville, Earl of Warwick. 1471: their sons, Richard (Warwick the Kingmaker) and John were killed at the Battle of Barnet. 1507: new house built by Sir John Cutte, Treasurer to Henry VII and Henry VIII. 1550: new house built. Seventeenth century: it is said tunnels were built during the Civil War to hide Royalists. 1669: bought by Sir Jeremy Snow, who built today's Jacobean gabled manor house, with massive chimneys, surrounded by a moat. Charles II and Nell Gwyn are said to have stayed here. Nell Gwyn's cottage in the grounds was the centre of a silkworm farm, which supplied the silk for Queen Elizabeth II's wedding

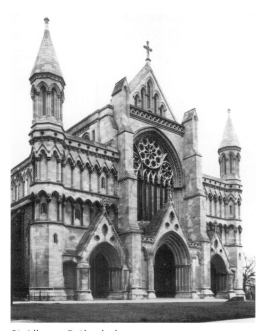

St Albans Cathedral.

and Coronation robes. 1702: Sir Jeremy Snow died and was buried in Shenley church. His nephew John Snell inherited. 1831: last of the Snell family died and the Hall was leased. 1905: Lady Randolph Churchill, as Mrs Cornwallis West, moved in. Her son, Winston, was a regular visitor. As he was by then in his 30s it is highly unlikely, contrary to the insistence of guide books, that the tree house belonged to him. 1939: de Havilland family home. The Mosquito design team was based here; the prototype was built in a fake barn behind the Hall. 1955: Hall taken over by ex-Royal Marine Major Walter Goldsmith, who restored it, opened it to the public and bought the prototype Mosquito to begin an Aircraft Heritage Centre, the first in the UK, with eighteen types of de Havilland aircraft on show. He sold the Hall in 1981. Now owned privately, the house is not open to the public but the museum behind the Hall is.

Sandon Farming village. Fourteenth-century church. Sandon Bury, seventeenth century, is said to have a dovecote of the same period. Jack Common, writer and journalist, lived here for five years and played dominoes in the Chequers pub. He was a close friend of George Orwell, who might never have moved into the county if not for Mr Common. Jack was assistant editor of the *Adelphi* magazine, based in the building of that name, for which Orwell wrote. Common said Orwell lived in poverty and looked like a tramp. Many letters survive between the friends. Jack and his wife Mary looked after Orwell's animals when he went to fight in the Spanish Civil War. Jack lived in 23 Hope Cottages (7 Payne End) until his wife, 40, died of cancer in July 1942. She is buried in an unmarked grave in Sandon cemetery. After that he moved to Datchworth* with their son Peter, aged 6.

Sarratt Old-world England. Traditional Hertfordshire village. If the name sounds familiar you are probably a Le Carré* fan because this is where he based his spy school. The name comes from a family called Syret who arrived from Scandinavia in 789. The Church of the Holy Cross has seen thirty-six monarchs come and go. Restored by Gilbert Scott*, who said the west window in the tower was older than Westminster Abbey. The distinctive saddleback roof is one of only four in England. The pulpit has been here since 1606. The door of the Cock Inn opposite the church is 3ft wide because the building was used as a mortuary for victims of the great plague of 1665. The village, now a mile from the church, probably relocated around the pond in the Middle Ages, when drovers stopped on their way to Barnet Fair.

Sawbridgeworth In Essex before the M11 motorway was built. Now known for Mr and Mrs David Beckham, it was once famous for one of Britain's oldest nurseries, opened by Thomas Rivers in 1725. Many new varieties of fruit were raised, including thirty varieties of plum. Peach trees were planted to commemorate Nelson's victory at Trafalgar. Son Thomas (1798–1877), a friend of Charles Darwin, built the Orchard House in Audley End. His rose gardens were famous. Only 'Rivers George IV' is still sold (Peter Beales Roses, London Road, Attleborough, Norfolk). A later Thomas Rivers bred the Conference pear, exhibited at the National British Pear Conference in 1885 – hence its name. It is now the most widely commercially grown pear in Britain. The nurseries run by the same family for 250 years, closed in 1985. Much of the land was bought for the Thomas Rivers Medical Centre, a private hospital, but the remaining apple, plum and cherry trees are looked after by Friends of Rivers Orchard.

Scott, Sir Gilbert George (1811–78) Architect of St Pancras Station, had relatives in the county and restored many churches here. He said he designed his first church, *Flaunden*, in 1838 because his uncle asked him to. 1853: *All Saints*, Garston; 1854: *St John's*, Bourne End; *St James'*, Thorley; 1856–77: *St Albans Abbey*; *St Stephen's*, St Albans – pews, stonework, east window, steeple; 1859: *St Katherine's*, Ickleford – south aisle and chapel; 1864: *Church of the Holy Cross*, Sarratt; 1866: *St Albans* clock tower; 1867: *St Mary's*, Childwick Green; 1871: *St James'*, Bushey – aisles and porch. *Holy Trinity*, Frogmore; *St Mary's*, Sawbridgeworth and *Orchard Mead Alms Houses*, Ridge, are also attributed to Scott.

Scott, John (1730–83) At Amwell* is a stone inscribed with part of his poem 'Emma'. Quirky, quixotic Quaker poet manqué, remembered not for poetry but for his Grotto in Ware, one of the finest in England, which took him thirty years to build. Some 34ft below ground and extending 67ft into the hillside are six rooms with walls lined with flints, fossils, minerals and thousands of shells from around the world. Restored in 1990, now on Scotts Road on a housing estate, it is open to the public every Saturday in summer. When his friend Dr Johnson* visited he said it was a 'Fairy Hall'. Commissioned William Blake to illustrate his self-published poems. Campaigned for animal rights, free education and against the death penalty. When the County Council was about to demolish his house, an irreplaceable early eighteenth-century architectural gem, the Amwell House Preservation Society was formed. Now a Grade II listed building, one window commemorates John Gilpin's famous ride from Edmonton to Ware, immortalised in a poem written by Cowper*. The house and grotto can be seen on Heritage Open Days.

Scott, Sir Walter (1771–1832) Novelist. Fascinated with the story of William Weare's murder, he visited Probert's Cottage in Radlett and was disappointed to find only parts of it remained. He paid a local woman 2*s* 6*d* to show him round. She told him it

Church of the Holy Cross, Sarratt.

had been knocked down as no one would live there. He stayed in Bushey and while there visited The Grove, Moor Park and Cassiobury.

Sculptors (selection) *Franta Belsky* (1921–2000): *Joyride*, mother and child bronze statue, Town Square, Stevenage. His bronze heads of Cecil Day-Lewis, the Duke of Edinburgh, Queen Elizabeth II, Prince Andrew and John Piper are in the National Portrait Gallery. *Sir Reginald Blomfield*: Abbots Langley War Memorial. *James Gibb*: Nell Gwyn monument, Tring Park; Little Berkhamsted War Memorial. *Stephen Elson*: *The Hart*, County Hall, Hertford. *Barbara Hepworth*: *Turning Forms*, Marlborough School, St Albans; *Mother & Child*, St Albans Girls' School; *Vertical Forms*, relief in Hopton-wood stone, University of Hertfordshire. *Edwin Lutyens**: Ashwell War Memorial. *Keith Maddison*: statue of Sir Geoffrey de Havilland, University of Hertfordshire. *Henry Moore**: pair of heads flanking tower doorway, St Andrew's, Much Hadham; *Family Group*, Barclay School, Walkern; St Albans Abbey south transept, single

Family Group by Henry Moore at Barclay School, Walkern.

standing figure; Temple Wood School, Welwyn Garden City. *Joseph Nollekens* (1737–1823): Millionaire miser, one of the strangest men ever. 1761: tomb of Samuel Burroughs, St Mary Magdalene, Offley*. Some books say the monument there of Sir Thomas Salusbury and his wife is also by Nollekens. It is thought he also carved some of the memorials in Holy Trinity, Throcking. *Charles Voysey**: Potters Bar War Memorial. *Kathleen Scott* (1878–1947), widow of Scott of the Antarctic, mother of Peter Scott the naturalist, close friend of Cherry Garrard*: 1930 bronze statue *Ad Astra* on brick plinth, Welwyn Garden City Campus.

Sebright, Sir John (1767–1846) MP for Hertfordshire. Animal breeder. In 1804, having built Sebright's London home, Sir John Soane designed Beechwood in Flamstead* (now a school) for him. Capability Brown designed the gardens. Maria Edgeworth*, a frequent visitor, said he treated his animals like children and his children like animals. Remembered for founding the Library of Irish Manuscripts at Trinity College Dublin, donating his valuable collection of Welsh manuscripts to Hafod, a country house in Wales, and for a chicken. The Sebright bantam was the result of thirty years' intensive breeding and is now one of the oldest breeds. A friend of Charles Darwin and of Edmund Burke, who was passionate about Irish literature. Burke discovered in Sebright's library at Beechwood important early Irish manuscripts and sent them for evaluation to Trinity College Dublin. Sebright later presented them to the college library. He has a memorial in St Leonard's Church.

Second Oldest Shop in Britain (the oldest is The Jew's House, Lincoln, 1160). Timbers dendro-dated to 1297. Discovered inside

The second oldest shop in Britain.

173 High Street, Berkhamsted during conversion of Figgs Victorian chemists. A well was found and smoky timbers suggest the shop was used by a craftsman working with fire and water, such as a jeweller. A page from a sixteenth-century prayer book was also found in the wattle-and-daub walls. The timber frame is preserved within the building, which was converted into an office through a £250,000 grant from English Heritage. Open to the public on Heritage Days. Grade II*.

Sellers, Peter (1925–80) Film star. Lived in The Manor House, Chipperfield*, with his wife and children until he fell in love with Sophia Loren, who arrived at Elstree in the 1950s to film *The Millionairess* with him. His unrequited passion led to divorce. During the filming Loren's jewellery was stolen. In the 1990s a burglar sold his story to a national newspaper, admitting the theft.

Spike Milligan unveiled a British Comedy Society plaque at Elstree to mark Sellers's huge contribution.

Shaw, George Bernard (1856–1950) Playwright. 1906: he was waiting to buy a house in Harmer Green but the deal fell through so he rented the 1902 New Rectory, Ayot St Lawrence. After fourteen years he bought it and called it Shaw's Corner. Very interested in Letchworth Garden City, he bought shares in the scheme. He wrote 1,000 words a day in his revolving hut in the garden and walked into the village every evening. When he moved in, there was no piped water, gas or electricity in the village. This is where he spent his most creative years and wrote some of his most famous works, being awarded the Nobel Prize for Literature and an Oscar for *Pygmalion*. Every fortnight his chauffeur took him in the Rolls-Royce to Welwyn* to do his shopping and visit his barber. His ashes, with those of his wife, were scattered in the garden. Shaw left the house to the National Trust. It was opened by Dame Edith Evans.

Shenley Beehive-shaped eighteenth-century lock-up. Nicholas Hawksmoor lived in Porters. Eddie Chapman, wartime double agent, lived here. During the First World War the grounds of Porters became London

Porters, once the home of Nicholas Hawksmoor.

Colney aerodrome. 1924: Porters bought by Middlesex CC for a mental hospital; it was opened by George V and Queen Mary. 1939: many patients were moved elsewhere when it was taken over by the army. 1960s: an experiment in anti-psychiatry was undertaken. David Cooper, a follower of R.D. Laing, agreed to head the 2,000-bed hospital on the understanding that his unconventional approach to treatment might prove controversial. His patients were men aged between 15 and 30. In the 1980s 'care in the community' was introduced and patients were moved into hostels or sheltered accommodation. 1998: the hospital was closed. Porters is now divided into privately owned homes.

She Wolf of France The name the English gave to Isabella (1292–1358), wife of Edward II*, mother of Edward III*. 1308: came to England as a 12-year-old bride. She was humiliated when Edward and his lover Piers Gaveston kissed in public. She deposed her husband in favour of their son. Edward III gave her Hertford (including Bayford, Essendon and Hertingfordbury). She died in the castle.

Smallpox Dr Thomas Dimsdale (1712–1800) had a practice in Hertford and lived in Meesden Manor near Buntingford. He pioneered inoculation and published *The Present Methods of Inoculation for the Smallpox* in 1767. The following year he was invited with his son Nathaniel to Russia, during an epidemic there, to inoculate Catherine the Great and her family. She gave him £2,000 expenses, a fee of £10,000, an annuity of £500 and a diamond-set portrait of herself, and made him a baron. Nathaniel received the same title as his father and was presented with a diamond-encrusted gold snuffbox (Gilbert Collection, Somerset House, London). Smallpox struck terror

into poor and rich alike. Those infected were confined in Pest Houses to prevent whole communities being wiped out. The vaccine was discovered by a contemporary, Edward Jenner, who inoculated cowpox virus to build immunity against smallpox. The idea of inoculation was introduced into England by a contemporary of Dimsdale, Lady Mary Wortley Montague, who observed it in Turkey.

Smith, John (1798–1870) Rector, St Mary's, Baldock, for thirty-seven years from 1833. The poor son of a poor teacher, Smith was married, with a child, before he went (at 18) to St John's College, Cambridge. His wife was an invalid. 1818: after the publication of

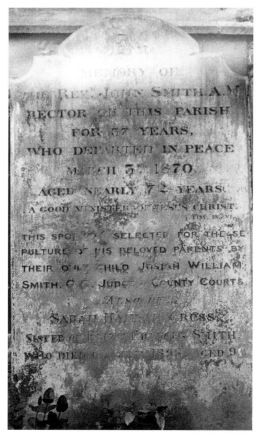

Grave of Revd John Smith, St Mary's, Baldock.

the Evelyn* diaries Lord Grenville paid Smith £200 to decipher those of Pepys. It took him four years of twelve-hour days. The diary cost 6 guineas and earned a lot of money for everyone except Smith, who was not acknowledged. He was living on a stipend of £130 p.a. Letters from Smith are in Pepys's library, as is the diary as he decoded it. At least he is recognised in death? No; his grave in a railed-off enclosure (with wife Elizabeth and son Josiah Smith, QC) is neglected. Maybe it is time for some Friends of John Smith?

Smith, Stevie (1902–71) Poet. Lived in Palmer's Green. Loved Hertfordshire and wrote about it in 'Brickenden', 'Freddy', 'Dear Karl' and 'The Ghost of Ware'. She often took the train to Hertford North with boyfriends for long walks, visiting pubs, teashops and churches. In 1928 she and Freddy broke into a deserted Camfield Place (later the home of Barbara Cartland*), which she said reminded her of houses in the books of Mrs Humphrey Ward*. Close friends included George Orwell and Louis MacNeice*.

Special Operations Executive (SOE) During the Second World War thirty-three mansions in the county were taken over by Section D of MI6, set up for espionage and sabotage operations behind enemy lines and nick-named Churchill's Secret Army or the Baker Street Irregulars (after Sherlock Holmes's group of spies).

Standon The Standon Stone is a lump of prehistoric Hertfordshire* puddingstone which is decorated on May Day. St Mary's Church has a detached tower, the only one in the county. The first Lord of the Manor, de Clare, fought with William I. A descendant founded Clare College*, Cambridge. The de Clares gave Standon to the Knights Hospitallers* in 1150. The Hospitallers' preceptory was where Standon Friars now stands; their flourmill was probably on the site of Papermill House. Their hospice became first a hospital and then a school. Names of surrounding fields include Knights Leys, Friars Lawn, Old Lawn and Balsams – the site of the Knights' herb garden. When Henry VIII closed the religious houses he gave Standon to Sir Ralph Sadleir, later a custodian of Mary, Queen of Scots. In 1561 Elizabeth I* stayed with Sadleir here on her way to Hertford Castle. Her visit cost him £1,920. A later owner was John Standon, so called because he was abandoned in the church porch as a baby. Brought up by the parish, he became a successful businessman.

Standon Green First* manned flight in Britain by Lunardi*, 12 September 1784, ended here. As he descended to the Green by throwing a grappling hook at a tree, hostile farmers attacked him with pitchforks.

Stevenage Britain's first New Town, loved and hated equally sixty years on. Six self-contained neighbourhoods of around 12,000 have their own schools, health facilities, shops, community centres and church. 1958: Franta Belsky's sculpture on Town Square unveiled by Sir David Bowes-Lyon, uncle of Elizabeth II. 1959: Queensway, Britain's first* car-free shopping centre, was opened by the Queen. 1980: Stevenage Borough Council formed. The Gordon Craig* theatre is the home of the English Sinfonia.

Stevenage, Old Mentioned in the writings of Defoe* and Pepys*. Childhood home of E.M. Forster*. Birthplace of Gordon Craig*, the son of Ellen Terry*. John Thurloe* farmed here.

Stocks Aldbury. First owner was called Stokkis. Its most famous inhabitant was novelist Mrs Humphrey Ward*. Now a

Stocks at Aldbury.

hotel, restaurant and golf club. The intelligentsia gathered here; Henry James, G.B. Shaw*, G.M. Trevelyan*, Aldous Huxley* *et al.* chewed over the problems of the day and debated Votes for Women (Mrs Ward was an opponent). In 1944 Stocks opened as a school. When it was closed in 1972 Victor Lownes, friend of Hugh Hefner, founder of *Playboy* magazine, bought it, built the largest jacuzzi in Britain and filled it with Bunny Girls. It was later owned by England cricketer Phil Edmonds. A picture of its swimming pool illustrated the cover of an album by the pop group Oasis.

Stone, Revd Samuel (1602–63) Puritan. Born in Hartford, as it was then spelled. 1633: emigrated to America and founded Hartford, Connecticut. His statue is near the entrance to Hertford Castle.

Stout Invented by Henry Stout, a Quaker maltster at the White Lion, Fore Street, Hertford.

Strange Last Resting Places Bramfield*, Brent Pelham*, Boxmoor Common*. Henry

Trigg, a Stevenage grocer, and Richard Tristram, a solicitor from Hollow Lane, Hitchin, were passing a churchyard at night when they saw bodysnatchers digging up the newly buried to sell to medical students. Horrified, they left instructions in their wills for their own burials. Henry ordered that his coffin be put in the rafters of his barn. 1724: his brother, the Revd Thomas Trigg, followed the instructions. 1769: his niece left money in her will for her uncle to be given a decent burial. 1831: the barn belonged to a pub; the landlord inspected the coffin and said Henry's body was still there. 1906: East Hertfordshire Archaeological Society viewed his skeleton. 1917: someone was said to have removed the bones of a horse. 2005: the coffin was still in the rafters (barn owned by NatWest Bank, 37 High Street, Old Stevenage). Is Henry still there? His friend Richard Tristram instructed his executors to buy land for his interment within the sound of running water. 1734: his son bought part of a field near Folly Brook, White Hill,

St Ippollitts. 1895: the land was sold. The grave, enclosed by an iron fence, is said to be still there near the Oakfield estate, close to the Stevenage to Hitchin road between Kingshott School and the Hitchin boundary, visible from the A602.

Straw In Victorian times no one was considered dressed without a hat and the county had a thriving industry (bonnets, boaters, sailor hats, panamas, etc.). Women who worked in hat factories earned £1 a week, more than farm labourers' 8s. Thousands more earned money by plaiting straw at home and in most villages straw-plait schools for children were set up. The beginning of the end came in 1865 when cheap plait was imported, although factories survived until the Second World War.

Sullivan, Arthur (1842–1900) Composer, famous for comic operas he created with W.S. Gilbert. He spent the summers of 1884, 1885 and 1886 at Stagenhoe near St Paul's Walden (now a Sue Ryder* Home). He paid £189 rent, which included valet, chef and three housemaids. After performing in London he would take the midnight train to Hatfield, then bribe the driver 14s to take him the extra 14 miles to Hitchin.

Sulston, Dr Sir John (b. 1942) Founding Director of the Wellcome Trust Sanger Institute. Brought up in Watford, where his mother was a teacher at Watford Grammar School. Sent to a local preparatory school, he won a scholarship to Merchant Taylors' School, Northwood. The Sanger Institute was a leading contributor to the Human Genome Project and is now devoted to using knowledge of genomes to further biomedical research. Dr Sulston was

Dr John Sulston, founding director of the Wellcome Trust Sanger Institute.

awarded a knighthood in 2001 for services to genome research and received a share of the Nobel Prize for Physiology and Medicine in 2002. His DNA is in a framed Petri dish in the National Portrait Gallery.

Synod Ecclesiastical council. 673: first* synod held at Hertford* to forge a national identity for the English Church. Representatives of the various churches agreed to unite and end disputes between Celtic pagan traditions and Christianity. Bede recorded the meeting between the five Bishops of the Kingdoms of England, called by the Archbishop of Canterbury, Theodore of Tarsus. Rules for determining the date of Easter* were set. Amazingly, this significant event was not commemorated until 1934, when a stone was placed in front of Hertford Castle.

T

Tate, John Opened the first* paper mill in Britain on the River Beane in Hertford in 1490. The first written reference to a paper mill in Britain is to Tate's. Chaucer's *Canterbury Tales* was printed by Caxton on paper from this mill. 1495: Tate supplied paper for a book printed by Caxton's assistant, Wynkyn de Worde. 1498: Henry VII visited the mill several times – it is listed in his household accounts. 1634: Henrie Kory purchased the mill. Sele Mill flats, near Hertford North station, now stand on the site.

Telegraph Hill Lilley. 600ft above sea level. The name comes from the wooden telegraph station built in 1808, linking the Admiralty in London to Great Yarmouth by semaphore telegraph. The Icknield Way* passes through this area of outstanding natural beauty. The land is privately owned; the Wildlife Trust has a management agreement with the owner. Home to rare wild flowers, butterflies and birds.

Templars Knights. 1142: King Stephen gave Dinsley near Preston (recorded as Deneslai in Domesday Book) to the Templars (some sources say he gave them Baldock at the same time, others that they received it only in 1185). It is said that before going on Crusade the Templars took their horses to nearby St Ippollitts'* to be blessed. 1185: given Buntas Ford (Buntingford). 1309: the Templars were disbanded; six Knights were arrested, two being sent to the Tower and four to Hertford Castle*. Edward II* was convinced they had buried treasure at Dinsley. The Templar properties were given to the Hospitallers*. Royston Cave is thought to have been used by them. 1860: a bricked-up room over the south porch of St Mary's, Baldock, was unsealed to reveal armour and pikes said to have belonged to Templars. 1880s: skeleton, chalice, and gravestone found near the east wing of Temple Dinsley, location of the Templars' chapel. 1909: thirteenth-century floor tiles found near the west wing. Inside nearby St Martin's Church is a thirteenth-century coffin lid from Dinsley. There is a defaced effigy of a Templar in Walkern church, beneath an arch on the south wall.

Temple Bar Famous county landmark 1888–2004. Because William I never conquered London he had to ask permission to enter the City, as does the monarch to this day. The Bar, marking the site of the symbolic gesture, is now in Paternoster Square, but from 1888 until 2004 was at Theobalds*. 1672: built by Wren after the Great Fire of London, it stood at the junction of Fleet Street and the Strand and was one of eight gates defending the City (Alders, Ald, Bishops, Cripple, Lud, Moor and New). 1878: dismantled because of traffic congestion. 1888: the wife of brewer Sir Henry Meux of Theobalds asked him to buy it for a grand entrance to the estate. It cost him £10,000. The Corporation of London bought it back in 1989 for £1. 2003: work started on dismantling the 2,700 stones by hand. The move cost £4m.

Temple Dinsley Preston. The Templars owned Dinsley until they fell from grace in 1309, after which it was given to the Hospitallers*. Sixteenth century: the Reformation. After Henry VIII closed the religious houses he gave Dinsley to Sir Ralph Sadleir. Eighteenth century: new house built. Between 1909 and 1922 Lutyens*

Princess Helena College, Preston.

added wings and outbuildings, first for the Fenwick family of department store fame. The gardens were laid out by Gertrude Jekyll*. 1915: bought by Douglas Vickers, the armaments manufacturer, who kept Lutyens on to complete the improvements to the property. He sold it to the Countess of Caernarfon, who sold it in 1935 to Princess Helena (third daughter of Queen Victoria) College.

Ternan, Frances In 1864 Frances, sister of Ellen (secret mistress of Charles Dickens*) lived in Waltham Cross with the Trollope family. When the wife of Anthony's brother Tom died suddenly in Florence, Anthony gave their daughter a home and arranged for Frances to give her music lessons. When she returned to Italy Frances went with her and married Tom.

Terry, Ellen (1847–1928) Actress. May 1868: following a disastrous marriage to famous painter G.F. Watts – she was 16, he was 47 – she left the stage and eloped to a cottage on Gusterd Wood Common near Mackerye End with a widower, architect Edward Godwin. She said her six years in Hertfordshire were the happiest of her life and that if Godwin had not got into financial difficulties she might never have returned to the stage. Edith, one of her two illegitimate children, born at Gusterd Wood in 1869, was delivered by Dr Rumball, the local doctor. Rumball had died by the time Edward (Gordon Craig*) was born in 1871. Godwin bought 20 acres at Fallows Green, Harpenden, and built a large house (now Pigeon Wick estate). 1873: bailiffs were knocking at his door. 1874: a desperate Ellen, visiting friends in Gusterd Wood, was careering down the lane to Batford Mill when a wheel came off the pony trap as the hunt was going by. She was recognised by theatrical entrepreneur Charles Reader, who persuaded her to return to the stage for £40 a week. 1877: after Watts divorced her for adultery she married not Godwin, but Charles Wardell. 1907: she married James Carew in Pennsylvania but ended up with Henry Irving and became Shaw*'s muse.

Tewin Water After Lady Cathcart's* death in 1783 Lord Cowper demolished the house and built a new one. Repton designed the gardens, which involved diverting the river and the road (now the B1000). Many have lived here since, the most famous being the Beit family, diamond merchant friends of Cecil Rhodes*. Sir Otto Beit was a keen cricketer and had his own ground and team. He also had his own fire brigade. 1950: Hertfordshire County Council made a compulsory purchase order (the house was occupied by a Mrs Drapes who allowed her hounds the run of the house). 1953: converted to a school.

Theobalds Sometimes pronounced Tibbalds. 1563: rebuilt by William Cecil, Lord Burghley, Secretary of State to Edward VI, Elizabeth I and James I. Elizabeth visited eight times, once for six weeks, to hunt deer, boar, hare and wolves. Each visit cost £700,000. James loved the place (he died here) and 'persuaded' Robert Cecil to swap it for the old Bishop's Palace in Hatfield. Raved over by John Evelyn* and visited by George Fox*, founder of the Quakers. It was destroyed by Cromwell. 1763: George Preston MP built a new house. 1841: bought by Sir Henry Meux*, London brewer. 1885: Sir Henry and his wife, Lady Valerie, built a new entrance using Temple Bar*. 1910: Lady Meux died and left her fortune to Admiral Sir Hedworth Lambton (1856–1929), on condition he changed his name to Meux. He sold the contents, including the carved Elizabethan oak staircase. 1929: Sir Hedworth died; his widow sold the property. 1937: house (Temple Bar excluded) sold to Middlesex County Council. 1939: requisitioned by Metropolitan Police Riding School. 1951: Borough of Enfield used it as a school. 1969: school closed. 1980s: used as adult education centre and conference centre 1990: restored.

Therfield Overlooks the Cambridgeshire plain. Houses date from the sixteenth and eighteenth centuries, including The Limes and Tuthill Manor. Prehistoric (4000 BC) long barrow unique in Hertfordshire, and round barrows from 2200 BC. Iron Age earthworks (700 BC) levelled by Italian POWs for potato planting. The Great Bustard, 2ft 6in tall, wingspan 7ft, the heaviest flying bird in the world, was common here until hunted to extinction. It is now being reared again in Salisbury. Stuffed specimens can be seen in the Zoological Museum*.

Thrale, Hester (1741–1821) née Salusbury. Niece of Judge Sir Thomas Salusbury of Offley*, friend and patron of Dr Johnson*. Married into the Thrale family of Hertfordshire. There is a monument of John Thrale in St Albans Abbey. His descendant Richard Thrale lives in Sandridge. The family acquired the lease to Sandridgebury (Thrale's End, Sandridge) from St Albans in 1309 and were appointed Victuallers to the monastery. There is also a Thrale's End Farm at Kinsbourne Green near Harpenden.

Thurloe, John (1616–68) Secretary of State under Cromwell*, had a farm at Old Stevenage*. Known as Thurloe's Farm until the 1930s, then the Cromwell Hotel, it is now the Corus Hotel, High Street. Thurloe was in charge of intelligence to root out those plotting against Cromwell. At the Restoration his life was spared in exchange for secret government documents.

Townsend, Peter (1914–95) Group Captain. Educated at Haileybury*. Battle of Britain hero, lover of Princess Margaret. 1940: DFC. Command of No. 85 Squadron at Hunsdon. 1941: squadron converted to night-fighting operations. His was the first night kill. 1942: mentioned in despatches,

Site of John Thurloe's farm, Old Stevenage.

awarded a bar to his DFC and DSO. 1944: appointed equerry to George VI, serving until the King died. 1947: CVO (Commander of the Royal Victorian Order). 1952: in service to the Queen Mother. 1953: appointed Air Attaché in Brussels. 1956: retired from the RAF. Moved to France, where he died.

Trees Native: ash, beech, chestnut, cherry, elm, holly, larch, oak, silver birch. Oak is predominant, followed by ash and beech. The county's dry climate suits poplars, willows and walnuts. Little remains of the elms which once dominated the landscape. Notable collections on old estates where rare trees survive: Brocket Hall*; Cassiobury*; Cheslyn Gardens, 54 Nascot Wood Road, Watford; Clarence Park, St Albans; Knebworth House*; Stanborough Park, Welwyn Garden City; Wall Hall, Aldenham.

Trevelyan, George Macaulay (1876–1962) Historian. Chairman, National Trust. Lived at Kings Road, Berkhamsted. Wrote his *History of England* for friend and neighbour William Longman, the publisher. Other close friends were John Buchan* (children's godfather) and Mrs Humphrey Ward*. He married Janet Ward, who carried on her mother's work, establishing London Play Centres, as did her daughter, Mary Trevelyan

Moorman (1905–94). 1925: horrified to hear Ashridge* was to be sold to developers, Trevelyan wrote an article, 'Must England's Beauty Perish?' He spent six years raising £80,000 from the great and the good, including Stanley Baldwin, Ramsay MacDonald, Lord Asquith, Lord Grey, Buchan* and the Courtauld family who lived near the common, to help the NT buy 1,600 acres.

Tring Immortalised in Edward Lear's 'There was an old person of Tring'. Also famous for George Washington*, the Rothschilds*, the Tring Helmet (found in the canal in 1813) and the Tring tiles, now in the British Museum. 1835: London and Birmingham Company built a railway line alongside the canal. Robert Stephenson (1803–59), son of the famous George, devised a system of ramps, pulleys and horses to barrow out the spoil. It was 2½ miles long and 40ft deep. The railway was never intended to pass through Tring, but local businessmen petitioned the company to build a station, putting London within an hour's journey.

Tring Manor 1680: Charles II gave it to Henry Guy (1631–1710), Secretary to the Treasury and spy for Charles and his brother James. 1682: Guy built a new mansion designed by Wren and, it is said, a house in the grounds for Nell Gwyn*. One of Guy's tenants was the Revd Lawrence Washington*. After Charles II's death Parliament sent Guy to the Tower, convicted of bribery. William III stayed here in 1690 and in 1705 sold the Manor to the Lord Mayor of London, Sir William Gore, who had the grounds landscaped by architects Charles Bridgeman and James Gibbs. There is an obelisk dedicated to Nell Gwyn, with lovers' graffiti from the 1740s. 1872: the Manor was sold to the Rothschilds for £230,000. The house, incorporating Wren's house, was enlarged to accommodate guests such as the Prince of Wales, PM Gladstone and Lord Rosebery. Walter Rothschild, whose 21st Birthday Avenue runs from the house, is remembered for stocking the park with rare animals and building the Zoological Museum*. During the Second World War the Manor was home to the Rothschild Bank. After the war the Arts Educational School moved here from bombed-out London and sold part of the park (Mansion Drive).

Tristram Shandy By Lawrence Sterne (1713–68) The narrator's 'uncle Toby', an ex-soldier with a thigh wound who spends his days reconstructing battles on his bowling green, is said to be Captain Robert Hinde (1720–86) of the Light Dragoons of Preston Castle. He put up battlements, built a drawbridge and had cannon on the front lawn. Followed by his 'army' (farmhands and village children) in a uniform of his own design, he would march to Hitchin with drum and trumpet, proclaim from the square the anniversary of a battle and on return fire a salute.

Trollope, Anthony (1815–82) Novelist. Hertfordshire roots on his father's side go back to the 1600s. Named after his grandfather, Rector at Rushden*. 1859: moved to Waltham Cross, where he lived until 1871. Blissfully happy, and retired from the Post Office, he completed the Barset Chronicles and started The Pallisers. Waltham Cross Sorting Office stands on the site of his old house: very fitting.

Trollope, Fanny (1780–1863) Married Thomas Trollope, barrister on the Hertfordshire circuit. Although the assizes and quarter sessions were held at Hertford, he was so unpopular he got few briefs. His father was the Revd Anthony Trollope, Rector of Rushden*, his mother was the (old) squire's daughter. Because her brother (the new squire) was a childless widower, she expected to inherit Julians, the manor house. However, aged 65, her brother unexpectedly married again and had five children, cutting the Trollopes out of his will. The financial blow blighted the family, and Fanny took up writing at the age of 50 to earn some money. Anthony Trollope's* novels are about property, inheritance, money or the lack of it.

Tudor, Catherine (d. 1437) Following her forbidden marriage to Owen Tudor, the pregnant Dowager Queen of Henry V was befriended by Bishop Gray of London, who took her to the Bishop's Palace, Much Hadham, to have her baby, known as Edmund of Langham, in secret. Edmund was the father of Henry VII. All Saints', Hertford, has a brass of her chef, aptly named John Hunger (d. 1435). 1436: Edmund and Jasper of Hatfield, her sons by Owen Tudor, were taken from her. She was confined to Bermondsey Abbey, where she died the following year, 3 January 1437.

Tudor, Edmund (1430–56) Born in secret at the Bishop's Palace, Much Hadham*, summer retreat of the Bishops of London for 900 years. Edmund of Hadham was the first* of the House of Twdr (anglicised to Tudor). Had he not been killed in battle, would he have become Edmund I? 1453: his half-brother Henry VI officially declared him legitimate and made him Earl of Richmond. 1456: died in captivity in Carmarthen Castle. His 13-year-old bride Margaret Beaufort* was pregnant. Henry is a royal name. Foregone conclusion that he would become Henry VII?

Tudor, Jasper (1431–95) Born in Hatfield, known as Jasper of Hatfield. Second son of Owen Tudor and Catherine de Valois. Legitimised by his half-brother Henry VI, who made him Earl of Pembroke after First Battle* of St Albans. Fought with his nephew Henry Tudor (Henry VII) at Battle of Bosworth.

Tudor, Owen (or Twdr, Owain) (1400–61) Hertfordshire launched the Tudor dynasty, one of the world's most famous. A default dynasty. Owain ap Maredudd ap Tudur/ Twdr, born in Anglesey into an old landed family, was named after his father's cousin, Welsh prince and hero Owain Glyndwr. As a lad he was sent to the court of Henry V to fight in France and was present at Henry and Catherine's marriage. After Henry's death Catherine was given Baynard's Castle in London, where she secretly married Owen in 1428, while an Act of Parliament was being passed to make it a serious offence to marry a Dowager Queen without the consent of the King (who was 1 year old). Owen was put in Newgate prison. When Catherine died he was summoned before parliament but refused to go without written safe-conduct and took sanctuary at Westminster. He was allowed to return to Wales only to be brought back and again put in Newgate prison. He managed to escape but was caught and imprisoned in Windsor Castle, but was released the following year. His stepson Henry VI, who had by then come of age, liked him and gave him an annuity. Owen, loyal to Henry, was taken prisoner at the Battle of Mortimer's Cross (February 1461) and executed. When his head was put on the market cross, a local woman washed his face and combed his hair. He was buried in the Church of the Grey Friars, Hereford.

Tyttenhanger Coursers Road, Colney Heath Ridge near St Albans. In the eighth century Offa* gave it to the abbots of St Albans. 1528: Henry VIII with Catherine of Aragon and their retinue moved here while the sweat raged in London. 1547: Henry sold it to Sir Thomas Pope (1507–59), who redesigned it, incorporating stained-glass windows taken from St Albans Abbey. Pope, who founded Trinity College, Oxford, managed to keep his head when all around were losing theirs during the reigns of Henry VIII, Edward VI, Mary Tudor and Elizabeth I. Tyttenhanger was inherited by relations of Pope's second wife (from the Blount family; they took the name Pope Blount). 1652: new house built. 1723–1856: occupied by members of the Pope Blount and Yorke families. 1755: Charles Yorke, Chancellor, married the sister and heiress of Sir Henry Pope Blount. Their son was Lord Hardwicke. 1811: the Earl of Caledon married Lord Hardwicke's daughter, Lady Catherine Yorke. 1857: Earl Caledon built a new house. His son, Harold Alexander* of Tunis, spent childhood holidays and part of his honeymoon here. He was buried in St Margaret's, Ridge. 1898: the Earl died when Harold was 6 and his brother inherited. 1939: Harold's mother died. 1973: the Caledons sold the estate to the John S. Bonnington architectural practice, whose sensitive conversion of the house won a European Architectural Heritage Year Award.

U

University of Hertfordshire A new university with new ways. 2,000 staff. Its amazing Sports Village is open to the public. Honours ex-students such as Sanjeev Bhaskar and ex-residents such as folk singer Donovan. Commissioned *The Last Judgement*, a stained-glass window featuring the Beckhams *et al.*, questioning society's obsession with celebrities. Then there's Professor Fletcher's 'no diet-diet'; the best teaching observatory in Britain at Bayfordbury, where astronomers work with international teams (Rock God Brian May is a huge fan); Britain's first* Professorship in Public Understanding of Psychology: Chair held by Professor Richard Wiseman, ex-magician. His unit researches topics such as the psychology of luck, deception, the paranormal, lying, criminality, extra-sensory perception. Its LaughLab, an international study of humour involving 350,000 people from 70 countries, featured as a cover story of the *New Yorker*. The Unit provides training in the detection of deception to banks, law firms and fraud investigators. *Guinness Book of Records 2001*: Most Systematic Study into Haunted Locations; Largest Internet Joke Vote.

V

Van Gogh, Anna (1853–90) Sister of the painter Vincent. 1874: Anna worked in Miss Applegarth's School, Ivy Cottage, next to the Wellington pub in old Welwyn from August 1874 to December 1876. Too poor to pay for transport, Vincent sometimes hitch-hiked from London to stay with her at Rose Cottage in Church Street (plaque). In the Van Gogh archives are many letters they wrote from here to their brother Theo.

Victoria, Queen (1819–1901) Three of her PMs came from the county. Sometimes visited Dowager Queen Adelaide, widow of William IV, at Cassiobury. 1841: stayed with

Lord Melbourne at Brocket. 1844: stayed with William Wilshere at The Frythe, Welwyn. 1846: spent a weekend at Hatfield House to attend a state ball. The royal procession left Cassiobury for Hatfield after lunch, accompanied by two companies of Herts yeomanry, Lord Salisbury, the Duke of Wellington and Lord Cecil. Four triumphal arches were built at Hatfield, where a band played the national anthem. Legend says she refused to stay on the royal train while it crossed Digswell Viaduct and so was taken to the other side by carriage. 1851: when the royal train stopped at Hitchin on its way to Balmoral, William Ransom, a lavender farmer, presented her with a bottle of lavender oil.

Voysey, Charles (1857–1941) Architect. RIBA Gold Medal Arts and Crafts. 1899: designed The Orchard, his home in Chorleywood* (world famous). Also designed Hollybank in the same road for the local GP and a nine-bedroomed house in Shire Lane (sold in 2005 for £1,650,000). He designed the interiors, including furniture, fabrics, tiles, metalwork, doors, windows, fireplaces, hinges, latches, locks and keys. All are Grade II-listed buildings.

Rose Cottage, Welwyn, once the home of Anna Van Gogh.

Wadesmill The first* village in the UK to have a turnpike after a 1663 Act of Parliament demanded one on the Great North Road between Wadesmill and Royston.

Wain, Louis (1860–1939) The Cat Man. His paintings are now sold for £20,000 but he died penniless in Napsbury Asylum, St Albans. In 1927 a visitor noticed him doodling in the pauper's ward of Springfield Asylum, Tooting, where he had been for five years and told him he drew cats like Louis Wain. 'I am Louis Wain,' the patient said. The shocked admirer launched an appeal fund, led by a radio broadcast by H.G. Wells. Mr Wain was immediately transferred to Bethlem Royal Hospital, where he was given a private room while awaiting a place at Napsbury, a beautiful house in its own grounds. He was admitted on 30 May 1930 and after many happy years still drawing cats he died of a stroke. The mirrors he decorated for Christmas are still there.

Walkern Dubbed Walk On. The mile-long, single street is lined with cottages and Georgian houses. Alongside the White Lion stands a seventeenth-century dovecote, one of only three in the county. In the church, beneath an arch on the south wall, is a defaced effigy of a Knight Templar. Walkern will always be associated with so-called witch Jane Wenham. The Church claimed witches existed, as did the law, which was not repealed until 1736. Accused of witchcraft in 1713, Jane was the last to be condemned to death for its alleged use. Tried at Hertford Assizes, she pleaded guilty, but the judge reprieved her. When Jane received a free pardon from Queen Anne, John Plumer of New Place*, Gilston, invited her to live rent-free in a cottage on his estate, where she died aged 70. The dubious accolade of the last convicted witch in England goes to Helen Duncan, convicted and jailed during the Second World War.

Wallington, Eric Blair (1903–50), the author George Orwell, spent the happiest days of his life here where all his dreams came true. Had it not been for the war he would probably have died here. From 1936 to 1946 he rented a cottage here and kept chickens, geese and goats. This is where he got married (his wedding certificate is on show in the church), and where he was living when *Keep the Aspidistra Flying*, *The Road to Wigan Pier*, *Homage to Catalonia* and *Coming Up for Air* came out. It was here he had the inspiration for two of the world's most influential books, *Animal Farm* and *1984*. Wallington is as pretty today as it was when he lived here. If he came back he would see it hardly changed (only two houses have been built). The Plough Inn

The cottage where George Orwell lived in Wallington.

next door, where he had his wedding reception, is now a private house. Manor Barn, inspiration for *Animal Farm*, is also still here, as it has been for hundreds of years, still owned by the Wallace family.

Waltham Cross Built by Edward I* in 1292 in memory of his beloved Eleanor, marking the overnight stopping place of her funeral cortège on its way to Westminster Abbey. 1625: Charles I was proclaimed king at the gates of nearby Cedars Park. Most famous resident was Anthony Trollope*. The last public hanging in the county was said to have been here in 1914.

Walton, Izaac (1593–1683) Knew the county well and loved it. His wife, born here, was the half-sister of Bishop Ken* of Little Berkhamsted. He wrote *The Compleat Angler* in 1653 (never out of print). The book opens on May Day with a fowler, a hunter and a fisherman comparing hobbies as they walk along the Lea. They sing, recite poetry, recall country folklore, recipes and anecdotes about fishing. Walton used the Thatched House, Hoddesdon*, as his base.

He also fished at Amwell* and stayed at the Fish and Eels, Dobbs Weir, Hoddesdon.

Ward, Mary Mrs Humphrey Ward (1851–1920). Novelist and social worker. Daughter of Thomas Arnold, granddaughter of the famous Matthew Arnold of Rugby. Her husband Thomas was art critic for *The Times*. Bought Stocks* in Aldbury from Lord Grey and lived there twenty-eight years until she died. She is buried in the churchyard. Her feckless, indulged son, Arnold, Conservative MP for Watford, a compulsive gambler, lived off his mother yet played a significant role in the House of Commons to prevent women getting the vote. Mrs Ward's last years were dominated by worries over his massive debts. After she died, in order to pay off Arnold's creditors, his father had to sell her beloved Stocks. Her daughter never forgave Arnold and managed to write a biography of her mother without mentioning her brother.

Ware The Great Bed*, Scott*'s Grotto. For years the centre of England's malting industry. When Ermine Street, the main

Fish and Eels pub, Dobbs Weir, Hoddesdon, where Izaac Walton stayed.

The famous gazebos of Ware.

road of medieval England (Chaucer mentions Ware twice in *Canterbury Tales*), became the Old North Road, canny locals routed it through the High Street so that travellers to Lincoln, York and Scotland had to pass through. To service them, inns were built with beautiful gazebos overhanging the river. The George (1439), 29 High Street (Barclays Bank), was famous for its eel pies, enjoyed by Samuel Pepys*, Daniel Defoe* and Izaak Walton*, who all stayed there. 14 July 1553: Lady Jane Grey, aged 16, was proclaimed Queen of England by the Marquess of Northampton. She reigned nine days before being executed. 1647: Corkbush Field Mutiny. Having won the war for parliament, the New Model Army was furious it was to be disbanded without settlement of arrears of pay. The war would, Cromwell had said, give 'common people' the chance to be heard. The Levellers, led by Colonel John Lilburne, demanded a constitution and a biennial parliament chosen by manhood suffrage. Four troopers were cashiered for mutiny. One, chosen by lots, Private Richard Arnold, was shot. Discontent about arrears of pay persisted. The demand for universal suffrage was not achieved for another 280 years (1928).

Washington, George (1732–99) Registers for the Church of St Peter and St Paul, Tring, have entries for the ancestors of America's first President. 1633: Revd Lawrence Washington, Rector of Purleigh, Essex, married Amphyllis Twigden, stepdaughter of Andrew Knowling of Tring. They had six children. 1642: Cromwell deprived Lawrence of his living for being a 'malignant royalist'. 1650: Andrew Knowling died, leaving £60 to Amphyllis, and to her son Lawrence a house in Frogmore End, which he owned until 1665. 1653: Lawrence Washington died. 1655: Amphyllis died. 1657: their eldest son, John, sailed for Virginia. His grandson, George, became America's first President.

Watercress Farms Once a huge industry, the last one left is at Nine Wells, Whitwell, near Hitchin. Purpose-built beds (no chemicals used) are fed with free-flowing pure spring water filtering up 250ft from an artesian well. Two crops a year are harvested in the traditional manner, cut and bunched by hand. The Sansom family has been here for 200 years.

Watermills Most villages had one. One surviving at Redbournbury near St Albans opens on Sunday afternoons. It sells organic stoneground, unbleached white, brown and semolina flours.

Waters, Elsie (1895–1990) and **Doris** (1904–78) Sisters of Jack Warner. Better known as Gert and Daisy, the original East Enders, wartime presenters and comediennes. Had art deco Blue Cottage built near Berkhamsted in 1938. Its semicircular façade and blue-tiled roof caused a stir. Showbiz personalities such as Diana Dors and Bob Hope stayed. The servants have gone but the bells that summoned them are still there. Their songs 'I've Got Sixpence', 'Goodnight Children, Everywhere', 'Kiss Me Goodnight Sergeant Major' were great hits. Their alter egos – chatty cleaners in overalls – bought them this beautiful home, a Bentley and Norman Hartnell (Queen's couturier) designer clothes. By 1959 they had fallen out of fashion until Ted Willis (who wrote *Dixon of Dock Green* for Jack Warner) created a TV show for them.

Watford Watling Street and a ford over the Colne. The Grove*. St Michael and All Angels has pre-Raphaelite stained glass by William Morris*, Ford Madox Brown, Philip Webb, Rossetti and Burne-Jones. Cassiobury*, home to the Earls of Essex, was demolished in 1927. A Turner watercolour in Watford Museum showing how it looked is enough to make strong men weep. The amazing oak staircase which took Grinling Gibbons three years to carve is in the Metropolitan Museum of Art, New York. Sir Geoffrey de Havilland* died at Watford Peace Memorial Hospital. Mo Mowlam* MP was born here. Sir John Sulston's* mother was an English teacher at Watford Grammar School. This is where Britain's first animated film, of Orwell's *Animal Farm*, was made in 1954 by Watford-born-and-bred Joy Batchelor (1914–91). Some 100 staff took three years to make the masterpiece and put the studios on the world animation map. She also made *Tales of Hoffnung*, narrated by Peter Sellers, *Automania*, and the first cartoon opera, Gilbert and Sullivan's *Ruddigore*.

Watford Gap The first motorway service station in Britain (M1) is nowhere near Watford, and not in Hertfordshire; it is 50 miles north, named after the tiny Northamptonshire village of Watford Gap on the B5385 just outside Daventry.

Watton-at-Stone Takes its name from a (small) lump of Hertfordshire* puddingstone outside the Waggon and Horses. In 1200, Lord of the Manor was Henry FitzAilwin, first Lord Mayor of London. During the Second World War, Frogmore Hall was Special Operations Executive* Station 18. The 'Sandringham Estate' in *The Lost Prince* was filmed in nearby Woodhall Park.

Waugh, Alec (1898–1981) Writer. With Inns of Court Officer Training Corps in Berkhamsted during the First World War. There is a memorial dedicated to the 12,000 men who trained here. 2,000 died. He married Barbara Jacobs, a local girl. Although the marriage did not last, his brother, the more famous Evelyn (1903–66), continued to visit the Jacobs family.

Welwyn St Mary's Church had two famous incumbents, Dr Young* and Samuel Johnes (1756–1852), who in 1785 refused to officiate at the illegal marriage between George, Prince Regent, and Maria Fitzherbert.

Aged 28, she was twice widowed, four years older than the Prince and a staunch Catholic. Theodore Hook, founder of *John Bull* magazine, was a frequent guest and wrote a ditty about Johnes, as he did of Welwyn. In 1828 Johnes inherited a large sum of money conditional on his changing his name to Knight. This is where Anna Van Gogh* lived. The 1960s were a great triumph for local archaeologist Tony Rook, who discovered a Roman* bath.

Welwyn Garden City Built in 1919, second of two in the county, the first being Letchworth. Following the ideals of social reformer Ebenezer Howard, it was planned with residents in mind, with plenty of open space, good-quality, low-density housing with gardens, local industry and amenities. 1922: Model Village built for *Daily Mail* Ideal Home Exhibition. Afterwards the houses were sold. One was bought by nuns. The same house later became the international headquarters of the Youth Hostel Association. 1926: Welgar (from Welwyn Garden) Shredded Wheat opened a factory. 1930: Lewis Grassic Gibbon (1901–35), aka James Mitchell, bought 10 Edgar Court. Later he bought 107 Handside Lane. He wrote seventeen books here in the seven years before his death. *Sunset Song* was dramatised by the BBC. He is revered in his home town of Arbuthnott, Kincardineshire, where there is a Lewis Grassic Gibbon Centre. His books are still in print.

Wendover Birthplace of Roger of Wendover (d. 1236), historian monk of St Albans. Also of John Colet (1467–1519), Dean of St Paul's, founder St Paul's School, friend of Erasmus and son of Sir Henry Colet, Lord Mayor of London, whose vast fortune he inherited. The place is synonymous with Rupert Brooke, who wrote about it in an oft-quoted poem. When he was at Cambridge University he would walk the 'Roman road to Wendover, By Tring and Lilley Hoo'.

Wesley, John (1703–91) Religious leader, took Methodism all over the county. His diaries often mention Barkway*, Barley*, Barnet, Hertford*, Royston*, St Albans*. He preached at Hertford at least ten times (plaque at 25 Castle Street). The town presented a mahogany pulpit to his chapel in City Road, London.

West, Dame Rebecca (1892–1983) Writer. Lived in Quinbury Farm, Hay Street, near Braughing. Mistress of H.G. Wells* and

Quinbury Farm, Hay Street.

mother of his son Anthony, born 4 August 1914. Spent part of her confinement in Wood Cottage Nursing Home, Chorleywood, and moved to Quinbury the following month. The pair called themselves Mr and Mrs West. The housekeeper hired by Mrs Wells despised Rebecca, stole from her and threatened blackmail. The same cart track still leads to Quinbury, which stands alone in the middle of fields. Wells chose it because it was hidden. He lived in Easton Glebe Rectory, a grand country house in Easton Park (Lady Warwick's estate), Little Easton, Great Dunmow. His playing the part of country squire with wife and sons bore no comparison to Rebecca's humiliation at Quinbury. In *The Fountain Overflows* her main character is Richard Quinbury. While here she wrote *Women of England*, describing her life. Wells spent Saturday and Sunday at Little Easton, Tuesday in London and the rest of his time here. He cycled here until he bought a car, and until the day he arrived to find the government had billeted soldiers here. Furious and jealous, he ordered Rebecca to move out, so in July 1915 she went to Royston Park Road, Hatch End, near old friends in Chorleywood.

Westmill Button Snap, Cherry Green, was inherited by Charles Lamb*. Mr Sargus was the tenant when Lamb wrote saying he had sold it. The Charles Lamb Society once owned it, but it is now privately owned. Plaque on the cottage. The medallion stone portrait of Lamb on the grass outside was rescued during demolition of a bank in Chancery Lane.

Wheathampstead Near headquarters of the Catuvellauni*. 54 BC: massive earthworks (Devil's Dyke) 130ft wide at the top and 40ft deep. Razed by Julius Caesar. Finds here include a 20 BC coin of King Tasciovanus. Excavated by Sir Mortimer Wheeler, he

Button Snap, Westmill.

found AD 10 bones of a woman and a child, AD 300 coins, a 628 Anglo-Saxon burial bowl and a bronze pot. 1312: the Barons assembled their forces here against Edward II* and Piers Gaveston.

Wheeler, Sir Mortimer (1890–1976) Archaeologist, star of popular TV archaeology programme *Animal, Vegetable, Mineral?* It was he who said the headquarters of Cassivellaunus* were at Wheathampstead*. He excavated the tepidarium and mosaic floor of a bathroom in a large Roman town house. It is now in St Albans museum. He also excavated the lake in Verulamium Park in 1929 before it was turned into a leisure area by Jarrow marchers.

Widford John Eliot (1604–90), founder of Harvard University, was born here. His father, Bennett, also owned land in Ware and Hunsdon. 1631: Eliot landed at Boston with his three brothers and three sisters. He began preaching in English to native Indians but within a year was using their language. 1640: translated Psalms of David into the Indian language Wampanoag, the first book in the language. 1654: the second building on Harvard campus is the Indian College. 1663: translated the Bible into Algonquin. It was printed by Harvard Press, and was the first Bible to be published in America. Many were shocked it was not in English or indeed in any European language. It was to be 120 years before the first Bible in English was published in America. In the nineteenth century Charles Lamb* wrote about his beloved Blakesware (demolished) in Widford, where he stayed with grandmother Mary Field, housekeeper to the Plumers. He remembered gazing at the busts of the Caesars and at Hogarth prints on tapestry-covered walls. The busts were taken to New Place* (also demolished). Colonel John Plumer died in 1719, leaving Blakesware

and New Place to his son William, MP for Hertfordshire, who died in 1767. His widow continued to live at Blakesware until her death in 1778, after which it was seldom occupied. Mary Field is buried in the graveyard. The pub used to have Lamb memorabilia.

William I (1027–87) 1066: 'He devastated Hertfordshire and did not stay his hand from burning the towns to ashes or from slaughtering the people until he came to a town called Berkhamsted*.' It was here he built the first* of his ring of defensive castles around London. His Domesday Book lists five boroughs: Ashwell, Berkhamsted, Hertford, St Albans and Stansted Abbots. In his will he left Normandy to his first son Robert and England to his second son William. When Norman lords Hugh de Grandmesnil of Ware and Count Eustace of Tring and Braughing said Robert was also entitled to England, both lost their heads.

Williams, Charles (1886–1945) Writer. Brought up in St Albans. Friend of C.S. Lewis and J.R.R. Tolkien. The three would meet every Thursday in Lewis's Magdalen College rooms to read aloud from the books they were writing. They called themselves 'The Inklings'. Like Lewis's and Tolkien's books, his had a religious message. Theirs made them famous, his didn't. Tolkien said it was probably because Williams had an unhealthy obsession with black magic.

Wind Turbine The county's first*, 50ft high, alongside the M25, is in King's Langley on the site of the old Ovaltine* Egg Farm. The 1930s buildings were reused, with restrictions to protect the site's history. Renewable Energy Systems design, build and operate wind farms all over the world. Their headquarters here at Beaufort Court is the first* zero emissions commercial office building in the world. The boiler is fuelled

Wind turbine on the old Ovaltine site.

by crops cultivated on surrounding land. Surplus electricity produced by the 225kW turbine is fed into the local grid, meeting the needs of thirty homes.

Wine Vineyards: Frithsden, Hemel Hempstead; Howe Green House, Hertford; Hazel End near Bishop's Stortford; Mimram Valley, Tewin Water, Digswell.

Wolsey, Thomas (1475–1530) Cardinal. Close personal friend of Henry VIII for twenty years until Ann Boleyn persuaded Henry to get rid of him. Lived at The Moor, as it was then known (Moor Park*). Some sources say Wolsey took out a lease on Delamere House, Great Wymondley. He also owned Cheshunt Great House, which survived until 1965. Its cellars are now sunken gardens surrounded by sheltered housing.

Wood, Sir Henry (1869–1944) Conductor. Founder in 1895 of the 'Proms'. Died in Hitchin Hospital. He had a grand funeral service in St Mary's, Hitchin, with the BBC Symphony Orchestra conducted by Sir Adrian Boult and the BBC Singers. During the war, after public concerts were cancelled and a flying bomb landed on his home, Sir Henry and the BBC Symphony Orchestra evacuated from London to Bedford. On the morning of 28 July 1944 he rehearsed all on the programme except Beethoven's Seventh Symphony, saying the orchestra was playing like a bunch of civil servants. After a perfect evening performance he became ill. His doctors, Skeggs (from Stevenage) and Lord Horder, were called. Dr Skeggs scoured the area for a nursing home but the only place with a bed was Hitchin Hospital, where Wood died. LNER put on a special return train for mourners from London. His first wife, Olga, was the daughter of a princess. After she died, he married Muriel Greatorex and moved into Apple Tree Dell, Chorleywood. The

Hitchin Hospital, where Sir Henry Wood died.

original plans for their Jekyll* garden are in the Museum of Garden History in London. The marriage ended in divorce. As his health was failing, his third wife was ostensibly his nurse. She was the singer Jessie Goldsack.

Woods Since 1920, 45 per cent of the county's woodland has disappeared. The Broxbourne National Nature Reserve, at 586 acres, is the largest in the county. It is owned and managed by the Woodland Trust and the County Council. It is classified as ancient woodland, which means continuously wooded from 1600, although in fact it has been cultivated since the Bronze Age (1000 BC). Home to rare species of wildlife.

Wymondleys Great and Little. Ley = lea/meadow. Land owned by a Saxon by the name of Wymond. Great, which is smaller than Little Wymondley, has thatched cottages, a Norman church, castle earthworks and the Elizabethan Delamere House which local legend says was leased to Cardinal Wolsey. It is also said that Henry VIII almost drowned here when his pole broke as he was vaulting a ditch. Little Wymondley, where Lucas*, England's most famous hermit, lived, has the moated Bury, seventeenth-century Hall, Georgian Wymondley House and Wymondley Priory (Augustinian, thirteenth century), where William de Arundel, biblical translator, was buried in 1246. The nave of the priory church, converted into a house after the dissolution of religious houses, is still lived in. Weddings are held in the huge oak barn built in 1541. Some of its timbers date from 1265.

Y

Young, Edward (1683–1765) Following three bereavements he wrote 'Night Thoughts', which launched 'The Graveyard' School of Poets (e.g. Gray's 'Elegy'). Rector of St Mary's Welwyn* for thirty-five years, he lived first at Mill Lane, then at Guessens. He founded St Mary's School, turned his rectory garden into a spa and built assembly rooms. His memorial in the church was commissioned by his son, who was visited here by Dr Johnson and James Boswell.

Z

Zeppelins So called in Germany after Count von Zeppelin, known as airships in the UK. 600ft long, hydrogen-filled rugby-ball-shaped balloons as large as a destroyer. January 1915: the first air raid on Britain had little military purpose, it was intended to undermine morale. 2 September 1916: the first* was shot down behind the Plough Inn, Cuffley, by 19-year-old Lt William Leefe Robinson, piloting an open cockpit bi-plane. Weeks later Lt Tempest shot down another over London; it ended up in Potters Bar (pieces are in the local museum). A newspaper reporter was on the spot within hours. In a barn were bodies covered with blankets. He pulled back the first blanket and identified the body immediately, having seen photographs of Zeppelin crews. It was Lt Heinrich Mathy, who held the record for the most bombing raids on Britain. Lt Tempest was promoted to Major and awarded the DSO. Lt Leefe Robinson was awarded the first VC for heroic action in Britain. A POW the following year, tragically he died of TB, aged 21.

Zoological Museum Tring. The house was given to Walter Rothschild* (1868–1937) as a 21st birthday present, subsequently given by him to the nation. If you want to see a komodo dragon or a flea in drag, this is the place. A serious speech impediment meant young Walter found it difficult to socialise. What saved him from a miserable life was his passion for natural history (and untold wealth of course). An eccentric, he drove a zebra-drawn carriage, commemorated in a mosaic in Tring town centre. He once drove it onto the forecourt of Buckingham Palace. He stocked his back garden with wolves, rheas, marabou, storks, dingos, kangaroos, kiwis, cassowaries, giant tortoises and *glis glis**, and planted giant sequoias among the beech, ash and yew, making it, to say the least, unique. Tring Park, now sliced in two by the bypass, is a Site of Special Scientific Interest (SSSI), the most important in the county for rare butterflies and plants. Walter would be pleased.

The Zebra Mosaic, Tring.

Resources & Further Reading

Central Resources Library, Travellers Lane, New Barnfield, Hatfield, Herts: biographies and autobiographies, many of which are out of print and not easily obtainable elsewhere.

Hertfordshire Archives: www.hertfordshire-genealogy.co.uk

Local Studies (HALS), County Hall, Hertford: indispensable site for researchers of local and family history.

Many of the places mentioned in the book have their own informative websites.

Aubrey, John, *Brief Lives*, Harmondsworth, Penguin, 2000

Beamon, Sylvia P., *The Royston Cave*, Baldock, Cortney Publishers, 1992

——, *Exploring Royston Cave: A Simplified Guide*, Royston, Royston and District Local History Society, 1998

Birtles, Philip, *Hatfield Aerodrome: A History*, Hatfield, British Aerospace, 1993

Bishop, Edward, *The Wooden Wonder*, Shrewsbury, Airlife, 1980

Blyth, Henry, *Caro: The Fatal Passion: The Life of Lady Caroline Lamb*, London, Hart-Davis, 1972

De Havilland, Geoffrey, *Sky Fever: The Autobiography of Sir Geoffrey de Havilland*, London, Hamish Hamilton, 1961

Hickman, Katie, *Daughters of Britannia: The Lives and Times of Diplomatic Wives*, London, Flamingo, 2000

Hine, Reginald, *Charles Lamb and his Hertfordshire*, London, J.M. Dent and Sons, 1949

Jackson, A.J., *De Havilland Aircraft since 1909*, London, Putnam, 1978

Le Carré, John, *Sarratt and the Draper of Watford*, Sarratt, 1999. (Available from HALS, County Hall, Hertford)

Myers, Jeffrey, *Orwell*, New York, Norton, 2000

Ogilvy, David, *DH88: The Story of de Havilland's Racing Comets*, Shrewsbury, Airlife, 1984

Ray, Gordon Norton, *H.G. Wells and Rebecca West*, London, Macmillan, 1974

Sharp, C. Martin, *De Havilland: An Outline of De Havilland History*, London, Faber & Faber, 1960

Smith, Graham, *Hertfordshire and Bedfordshire Airfields in the Second World War*, Newbury, Countryside Books, 1999

Turner, Des, *Aston House SOE. Station XI*. Available from the author, Richmond House, 2 Benington Road, Aston, Stevenage SG2 7DX

West, Anthony, *H.G. Wells*, London, Hutchinson, 1984

Wheeler, Sara, *Cherry: A Life of Apsley Cherry Garrard*, London, Vintage, 2002

Whitmore, Richard, *Of Uncommon Interest: True Stories and Photographs of Ordinary People and Extraordinary Events in Victorian and Edwardian Times*, Bourne End, Spurbooks, 1975

——, *Mad Lucas: The Strange Story of Victorian England's Most Famous Hermit*, [Hitchin], North Hertfordshire District Council, 1983

Acknowledgements

My thanks to:

Chris Reynolds of www.hertfordshire-genealogy.co.uk; friends Pat and Robin Webb for unlimited moral and practical support; Terry Ransome, Director, Publicity and Marketing, Hitchin British Schools Trust, Hitchin; Josh Tidy, First Garden City Heritage Museum, Letchworth; John Ely of Shenley. Special thanks to Robin who checked, amended and edited all my aviation-flavoured entries, drawing on his experience working at senior level in various aircraft companies at Hatfield from 1951 to the rundown of the site in 1992.

Local history societies, especially Abbots Langley, Bishop's Stortford, Chipperfield, Much Hadham, Radlett Redbourn, Rushden.
Hertfordshire County Council, especially Hertfordshire Archives and Local Studies, County Hall, Hertford.
District Councils, especially Dacorum and Hertsmere.
Tring Town Council.
Campaign for the Protection of Rural England (CPRE).

Picture Credits

Apart from those listed separately, all photographs were provided by Stuart Haden (www.stuarthaden.co.uk). He took the following with kind permission: The Priory, Hitchin (p.11); 'Torilla', Wilkins Green Lane, Hatfield (p.12); Balls Park (p.16); Great Nast Hyde (p. 21); Benslow House, Hitchin (p. 57); Hatfield House (p. 63); Mosquito Planes (p. 84); The Great Oak, Panshanger (p. 90); Wall carvings, Royston Cave (p. 99); Porters (p.105) ; Stocks at Aldbury (p. 108); Princess Helena College, Preston (p. 111); Quinbury Farm (p. 121); Wind turbine (p. 124).

Robin Webb for: One-hand turret clock (p. 29); Group Captain John Cunningham with de Havilland 'Moth' (p. 39); Statue of Sir Geoffrey de Havilland (p. 41); De Havilland Comet Racer (p. 42); John Walton, blacksmith (p. 67); Elizabethan wall painting, Much Hadham (p. 85).

Terry Ransome for The British Schools, Hitchin (p. 27); Faldo Enterprises for Nick Faldo (p. 52); Philip Waterson for Professor Stephen Hawking (p. 64); Roger Johnson, Editor The District Messenger (Newsletter of the Sherlock Holmes Society of London) for Sherlock Holmes (p. 70); Mrs Christiane Kubrick for Stanley Kubrick (p. 76); Spielplatzoasis for Britain's first naturist camp (p. 86); Richard Summers for Sir John Sulston (p. 109).

The following are from the author's collection: Witches' hat flues (p. 18); Charles Dickens (p. 43); Hertfordshire Spike at Ware (p. 68); The Old Rectory, Letchworh (p. 89).